MW00397806

THE FIELD GUIDE TO
TRAINS
LOCOMOTIVES AND ROLLING STOCK

THE FIELD GUIDE TO
TRAINS
LOCOMOTIVES AND ROLLING STOCK

BRIAN SOLOMON

VOYAGEUR
PRESS

Quarto is the authority on a wide range of topics.

Quarto educates, entertains and enriches the lives of our readers—enthusiasts and lovers of hands-on living.

www.quartoknows.com

© 2016 Quarto Publishing Group USA Inc.
Text © 2016 by Brian Solomon
Photography © 2016 by Brian Solomon, unless otherwise noted

First published in 2016 by Voyageur Press,
an imprint of Quarto Publishing Group USA Inc.,
400 First Avenue North, Suite 400, Minneapolis, MN 55401 USA.
Telephone: (612) 344-8100 Fax: (612) 344-8692

quartoknows.com
Visit our blogs at quartoknows.com

All rights reserved. No part of this book may be reproduced in any form without written permission of the copyright owners. All images in this book have been reproduced with the knowledge and prior consent of the artists concerned, and no responsibility is accepted by producer, publisher, or printer for any infringement of copyright or otherwise, arising from the contents of this publication. Every effort has been made to ensure that credits accurately comply with information supplied. We apologize for any inaccuracies that may have occurred and will resolve inaccurate or missing information in a subsequent reprinting of the book.

Voyageur Press titles are also available at discounts in bulk quantity for industrial or sales-promotional use. For details contact the Special Sales Manager at Quarto Publishing Group USA Inc., 400 First Avenue North, Suite 400, Minneapolis, MN 55401 USA.

Library of Congress Cataloging-in-Publication Data

Names: Solomon, Brian, 1966- author.
Title: The field guide to trains / by Brian Solomon.
Description: Minneapolis, MN : Voyageur Press, [2016] | Includes
   bibliographical references and index.
Identifiers: LCCN 2015047962 | ISBN 9780760349977 (flexi : alk. paper)
Subjects: LCSH: Locomotives. | Locomotives--History. | Diesel locomotives. |
   Railroad trains. | Railroad cars. | Railroad cars--History.
Classification: LCC TJ605 .S7747 2016 | DDC 625.2--dc23
LC record available at http://lccn.loc.gov/2015047962

10 9 8 7 6 5 4 3 2

ISBN: 978-0-7603-4997-7

Acquiring Editor: Todd R. Berger
Project Manager: Alyssa Bluhm
Art Director: James Kegley
Layout: Amy Sly

Printed in China

Front cover:
Canadian Pacific GP38-2.
Shutterstock

Back cover: (left) A Santa Fe GP60M crosses the California desert near Bagdad; (top middle) MBTA PCC streetcars pass at Milton, Massachusetts; (top right) Preserved Southern Pacific engine 4449 is one of AmericaÆs favorite 4-8-4s; (bottom right) Rolling pipeline: high-capacity tank cars carry California crude oil; (bottom middle) SEPTA Silverliner IVs catch the evening sun at Bryn Mawr, Pennsylvania. *Photos by Brian Solomon*

On the title page: A lone Chicago & Western Indiana RS-1 passes Rock Island RS-3s in Chicago. *Richard Jay Solomon*

MIX
Paper from responsible sources
FSC® C104723
www.fsc.org

TABLE OF
CONTENTS

DEDICATION

To Dan and Mary Howard

ACKNOWLEDGMENTS

Over the years, I've had countless discussions with railroad professionals all over the world regarding trains, locomotives, and their operations. I've combined this knowledge with a close study of railways at work and thorough reading on the subject. This book draws on information from more than sixty previous books I've written over the last twenty years, while filling gaps and highlighting new information. I've also provided a detailed bibliography, including a variety of Internet sources that I've consulted. Equipment manufacturers supply a great variety of technical detail on their trains in these sites, yet it helps to have an understanding of real-life applications to put these details into context. Although there is always the danger of error when publishing technical information, I've poured over a great deal of material in seeking out the correct data for this book, and it is my hope that it is informed and accurate.

Preparation of this book involved assistance and generosity from many people who lent me research materials, answered questions, provided transportation and lodging, and supplied photographs. Thanks to Chris Guss for helping with the text on GP33ECO units; and to Pat Yough for transportation, research assistance, photographs and introductions to other photographers. Tim Doherty supplied photographs and traveled with me on many occasions. Dan Bigda of the Boxcar Companies provided research and insight on freight car design, application, and fleet management. John Gruber helped with research and photography. Walter E. Zullig and Jack May provided tours of New York City area railways and supplied photographs. Scott Lothes, Tom Kline, Adam Pizante, Dan Howard, and Don Marson were generous with their photographic collections. Special thanks to my father, Richard J. Solomon, who offered photographs, brought me on my early railway trips (and supplied cameras and film), supplied source research, and proofread the text. The Irish Railway Record Society in Dublin gave me unlimited access to their research library. Thanks to Paul Goewey; David Hegarty; Denis McCabe; Bill Keay; Steve Carlson; Doug Moore; Mike Gardner; Rich Reed; Vic and Becky Stone; Doug Riddell; Isabelle Dijols; my brother, Seán Solomon, who traveled with me while I was researching and photographing for this book; and to my many friends who traveled with me in years past. Special thanks to Markku Pulkinnen, Petri and Pietu Tuovinen, Asko Räsänen, Mikko Tikkanen, Mauno Pajunen, Matti Mäntyvaara, Saki K. Salo, and Juhani Katajisto for Scandinavian travels as this book was in production. My late friend Robert A. Buck of Warren always deserves a mention—it was he who guided my interest in railways for many years, and who often lent me photographs and resources for my writings.

Thanks to my editor Todd Berger and project manager Alyssa Bluhm and everyone at Voyageur Press for making this book a reality. I know you'll enjoy it!

PART 1
Locomotives

INTRODUCTION

The diesel-electric locomotive is the standard motive power across North America. These locomotives can be grouped into several basic categories, but the most common is the road freight locomotive, which largely has been high-horsepower six-motor types since the mid-1990s. Smaller locomotive categories include switchers and passenger diesels. Among switchers are those with a modern arrangement called the *Genset* locomotive. Rather than a large diesel engine, these are powered by two or more low-emissions diesel gensets. (Each Genset is a complete self-contained diesel engine-generator combination.) In contrast to a large engine that must be running all the time, individual gensets are switched on only as needed to meet power demands. Since an onboard computer controls Gensets automatically, fuel consumption and emissions are much lower than with a conventional diesel engine that runs continuously.

Variations of the passenger diesel are dual-mode types: diesel-electric/straight-electric locomotives combined as a single locomotive. The classic General Motors Electro-Motive Division (EMD) FL9 is one of the best-known variations; modern types include a model variation of General Electric's GENESIS line, which, like the FL9, is designed to draw current from the line-side third rail. In North America, straight electrics are far less common than diesels and in recent decades have primarily been built for passenger services using adaptations of European designs.

After World War II, the diesel-electric dominated new locomotive sales across North America. General Motors emerged as the dominant builder and its locomotives largely set the standards for quality and service across the industry; in the United States, its Electro-Motive Division is typically listed as the builder and known by the initial EMD.

While EMD's carbody style diesels in the form of E and F units initially were the most common types of road diesels, it was Alco–General Electric's RS-1 road switcher that established common pattern, which ultimately dominated North American production. In the early 1950s, Alco and GE ended their partnership, and by the end of the decade, GE re-entered the heavy North American market on its own and in competition with its one-time partner. During the 1960s, EMD, GE, and Alco all built locomotives. Alco exited the business in 1969, although Montreal Locomotive Works, its one-time Canadian affiliate (later part of Bombardier), continued to build locomotives into the early 1980s. In the mid-1980s, General Electric overtook EMD as the leading locomotive builder. During the 1990s, EMD and GE introduced modern three-phase alternating-current traction systems, while focusing production on just a handful of high-horsepower road locomotives. In 2005, General Motors sold EMD, now part of Progress Rail owned by engine manufacturer Caterpillar.

The market for switching and passenger locomotives has changed. In recent years, newer, smaller companies have entered the business of building lower horsepower engines for switching and secondary service, often using primary components from recycled locomotives. In recent years, domestic and international locomotive manufacturers have engineered and sold passenger diesels for the North American market. MotivePower Industries MPXpress series of streamlined models emerged as a common type purchased by many suburban railroad operators. In other situations, various locomotive designs have been custom engineered for passenger work.

Chicago Metra was the only operator to buy EMD's F40PHM-2. *Brian Solomon*

PREVIOUS PAGE: The New Mexico Rail Runner has nine MP36PH-3Cs built by MotivePower Industries. *Tim Doherty*

Systems for locomotive model designations vary depending on the builder. Some manufacturers code output, traction type, and wheel arrangement details into their designations; others do not. There isn't much consistency between builders, and to complicate matters, designation systems tend to evolve over time. Furthermore, some builders use hyphenated designations, while others do not. In many situations, railroads have their own locomotive classification systems and may apply different locomotive designations than those used by the manufacturer. When locomotives are rebuilt or remanufactured, their designations are typically modified to reflect changes to horsepower and electrical systems. Generally, this book uses manufacturer locomotive model designation (or remanufactured model designation), and only acknowledges alternative designations when necessary to avoid confusion.

There isn't space to offer a complete spotter's catalog nor detailed rosters for all the variations and paint schemes of locomotives featured. However, in addition to the mix of common and specialized North American locomotives is a small sampling of European types, many of which are close cousins to locomotives working in North America.

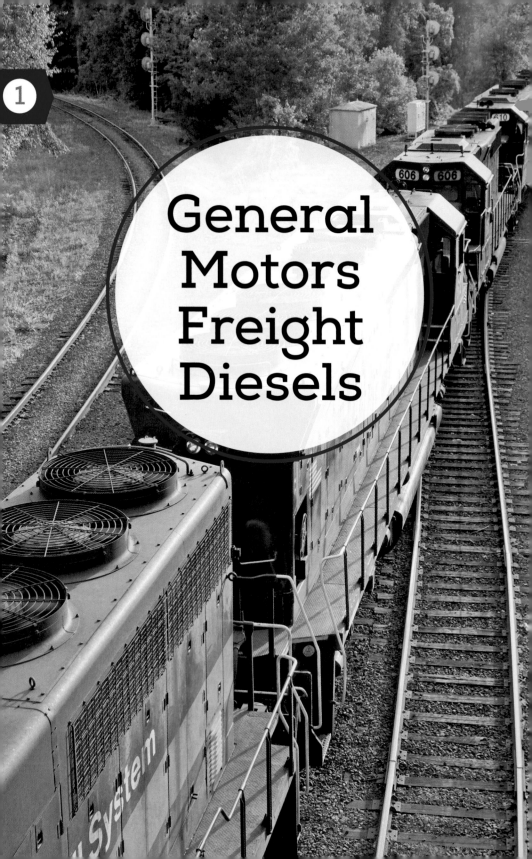

General Motors Freight Diesels

ELECTRO MOTIVE GP40

EMD's GP40 was a significant model type and one of the best-selling replacement diesels (known as the "second generation," since these locomotives replaced the diesels that had replaced steam). A careful examination is necessary to distinguish a GP40 from the variety of similar-looking EMD road-switcher models built between 1963 and 1994.

The GP40 was the first of nine EMD locomotive models introduced in 1965 that were based on the builder's new 645 diesel engine. EMD preferred a high-output two-stroke diesel engine design, which distinguished it from most other American locomotive manufacturers that used four-stroke designs. The 645 engine improved upon the proven 567 by enlarging the cylinder bore to increase total engine displacement from 567 cubic inches to 645 cubic inches (thus the engine designation). The new locomotive line also included electrical improvements designed to match increased engine output and provide better reliability. This included a new high-capacity traction motor and an AC/DC rectifier power transmission system (not to be confused with three-phase AC traction introduced in the 1990s).

The GP40 16-cylinder, turbocharged 645 engine generated 3,000 horsepower, and at the time New York Central took delivery of the first GP40s in 1965, the model was the most powerful American four-axle diesel and twice as powerful as the thousands of first-generation diesels

EMD GP40 SPECIFICATIONS

Type: B-B, diesel-electric road switcher

Manufacturer: EMD

Years Built: 1965-1971

Wheel Arrangement: B-B

Engine: EMD 16-645E

Output: 3,000 horsepower

Tractive Effort: 57,000 lbs. (varies depending on gearing/weight)

Max. Operating Speed: 65 mph with 62:15 gearing

Weight: 277,720 lbs.

Overall Length: 59 ft. 2 in.

OPPOSITE: Pan Am Railways operates some former SD45s, which still exhibit the classic "flared" radiator housing at the rear of the engine. *Brian Solomon*

BELOW: Florida East Coast 435 is an early production EMD GP40, built for Chicago, Burlington & Quincy in 1966. *Walter E. Zullig*

On November 7, 1987, Conrail 3050 GP40s roars west with a Trail-Van piggyback train at CP Draw in Buffalo, New York. *Brian Solomon*

at work on American railroads that were ripe for trade-in. The GP40 was intended to encourage railroads to replace older locomotives on a two-for-one basis. The GP40's high-horsepower output made it desirable for fast freight, especially intermodal trains that needed to get up to speed and cruise at 65 to 70 miles per hour.

EMD built 1,243 GP40s for North American railroads between 1965 and 1971 (at which time it introduced its Dash 2 line, with the similar-looking model GP40-2 that supplanted the GP40 in its catalog). Most GP40s were ordered for freight service, but EMD also engineered two passenger variations—models GP40P and GP40TC.

Many GP40s survive on American lines. These can be distinguished from similar EMD four-axle road switchers, such as the 2,500-horsepower GP35 and 2,000-horsepower GP38, by closely observing the exhaust fans on the roof at the rear of the car body: as-built, the GP40/GP40-2 models have three fans of the same proportions in a row. (The GP35's center fan has a lower profile, while the GP38 has just two fans.) The 1980s-era GP50 and GP60s have much larger radiator vents along with other external differences.

EMD SD45

Electro-Motive's more-powerful 645 engine was introduced in the mid-1960s and led to a variety of new models. The most powerful was the SD45, powered by a 20-cylinder 645E3 (turbocharged). The first production SD45s were built in 1966. EMD's earlier standardized locomotive lines essentially offered just one model for each major locomotive type, but the 645 line was a departure from this earlier philosophy and instead offered a variety of similar models by applying different 645-engine configurations. For applications where the SD45's 3,600 horsepower was too powerful, railroads had a choice of more conservatively powered SD40 and SD38 models.

By the 1960s, fast freight operations demanded higher horsepower, and the SD45 emerged as a popular locomotive.

SD45 SPECIFICATIONS

Type: Diesel-electric road locomotive

Manufacturer: EMD

Years Built: 1966-1972

Wheel Arrangement: C-C

Engine: EMD 20-645E3

Output: 3,600 horsepower

Tractive Effort: continuous 74,200 lbs. at 9 mph with 60:17 gearing)

Max. Operating Speed: 83 mph (with 60:17 gearing)

Weight: 407,000 lbs.

Overall Length: 65 ft. 9.5 in. or 65 ft. 8 in.

These 20-cylinder 3,600 horsepower SD45s locomotives were well suited to SP's heavy freight operations. *Brian Solomon*

ELECTRO-MOTIVE
DASH 2

General Motors' Electro-Motive Division introduced its Dash 2 line in 1972 as a marketing tool that allowed EMD to demonstrate that it had advanced its locomotive technology without radically changing its model designation system. Across its production, new "-2 models" replaced earlier equivalent models. The GP40-2 replaced the GP40, the SD40-2 replaced the SD40, etc., and in most instances were just improved variations of the earlier models. For the most part, horsepower output remained the same while reliability was improved along with other measures of locomotive performance. The most significant innovation was the introduction of a much more reliable electrical system that employed modular solid-state electronics to reduce the number of electrical components, and interchangeable modular electronic circuit boards that could be swapped out to simplify locomotive repair.

Some models, such as the GP38/GP38-2 and GP40/ GP40-2, looked nearly the same externally. Early in the production stage, only subtle equipment variations, such as the introduction of a rounded sight glass on the rear hood below the radiator intake vents, provided the clue that a locomotive was part of the Dash 2 family. However, during the course of Dash 2 production, EMD implemented new external equipment, such as a new style of radiator grill in place of the traditional variety that had been flush with the car body.

Other models had more pronounced differences. For example, the six-motor SD45-2 model is nearly 5 feet longer than model SD45. Also, where the SD45 featured distinctive angled radiator intake vents, the SD45-2 did not, and instead it had longer flush-mounted intakes. Model SD40-2 tended to use EMD's new HTC truck (sometimes spelled HT-C) in place of its earlier standard three-motor "Flexicoil" truck. Similar in appearance to the Flexicoil truck, the HTC used an improved motor arrangement, better dampening, and incorporated other innovations for more effective weight transfer and better adhesion. Externally, the HTC truck is most easily identified by the presence of a dampener on the second axle, resembling an automotive shock absorber. Another easy way to

EXAMPLE OF EMD DASH-2: SD40-2

Type: Road-frieght locomotive

Manufacturer: EMD and Canadian affiliates

Years Built: 1972-1986

Wheel Arrangement: C-C

Engine: 16_645E3

Output: 3,000 horsepower

Tractive Effort: 70,000 lbs. with 62:15 gearing*

Max. Operating Speed: 65 mph with 62:15 gearing

Weight: 368,000-390,000 lbs. depending on options

Overall Length: 68 ft. 10 in.

*higher continuous tractive effort figures are given when locomotives are equipped with advanced wheel slip control systems.

distinguish the SD40-2 was its longer platform measuring
68 feet 10 inches (a little more than 3 feet longer than the
SD40). As a result, SD40-2 truck centers are farther apart
than on the SD40. The SD40-2 was sold in large numbers
and by the mid-1980s had become the most common
locomotive in North America.

Florida East Coast 716, an
SD40-2 Dash 2 variation with
an elongated nose, was built
in 1980 for Union Pacific.
Brian Solomon

GMD GP40-2L

A Canadian variation of General Motors Electro-Motive Division's successful GP40-2 was built during the 1970s by EMD's Canadian subsidiary, General Motors Diesel. This variation is distinguished by a full-width nose section and the four-piece windshield common on Canadian-style safety cab locomotives, and has been variously described as model GP40-2L and GP40-2W. Canadian National bought them for freight, while Toronto's GO Transit bought eleven for passenger service. Some of Canadian National's units were cleared for international service and were regularly assigned to work Central Vermont, Grand Trunk Western, and its other American lines. Significantly, these locomotives were not equipped with dynamic brakes, which, combined with the awkward cab arrangement, resulted in relatively low resale value in comparison with other EMD four-motor types. Despite this, a number of smaller railroads in the United States have bought GP40Ls secondhand. New England-based Guilford Rail System acquired twenty of the type in 2000, while RailAmerica acquired several for work on its various properties. The Genesee & Wyoming empire acquired RailAmerica in 2013; since then, some of the GP40-2Ls have been handsomely painted in G&W's orange and yellow livery. Florida's Tri-Rail picked up a former GO Transit unit.

GP40-2L SPECIFICATIONS

Type: General-purpose diesel-electric

Manufacturer: General Motors Diesel

Years Built: 1973-1976

Wheel Arrangement: B-B

Engine: EMD 16-645E3 diesel

Output: 3,000 horsepower

Tractive Effort: 57,000 with 62:15 gearing

Max. Operating Speed: 65 mph 62:15 gearing

Weight: 260,000 lbs.

Overall Length: 59 ft. 2 in.

Vermont Rail System's Vermont Railway 311 GP40-2L (variously designated GP40-2W) is the former Canadian National 9662 that was painted in 2014 to commemorate Vermont Railway's fiftieth anniversary. *Walter E. Zullig*

A CSXT SD60M at Palmer, Massachusetts: this westward freight holds for a red signal at the end of the controlled siding at CP83 (dispatcher controlled point 83 miles from South Station, Boston) waiting for an eastbound train. *Brian Solomon*

EMD 60-SERIES

In 1984, Electro-Motive introduced a new line of 60-series diesels powered by its new 710G diesel to overcome limitations of its 1960s-era 645 diesel engine. Its best-selling new model, the six-motor SD60, externally resembles EMD's earlier SD50 , powered by the 16-645F diesel. The SD60 was rated at 3,800 horsepower, making it nominally more powerful than the SD50, but it was a significant step to greater reliability.

During SD60 production, EMD re-introduced the North American safety cab to the US Market. From the early 1960s to 1989, road-switcher models with what is now called the "conventional cab" had been standard. Notable exceptions were EMD's cowl types of the late 1960s, such as models F45 and FP45, and the massive eight-motor DDA40X (built solely for Union Pacific) that featured a wide-nose cab style. In the early 1970s, Canadian National's order for wide-nose cab locomotives set a precedent in Canada and ultimately led to the modern North American safety cab, which were introduced to the United States as result of changes to train-crew practices in the mid-1980s, that included the phasing out of the fireman's position, elimination of caboose operation, and lengthening

EXAMPLE OF EMD 60-SERIES: SD60

Type: road freight locomotive

Manufacturer: EMD

Years Built: 1984-1991

Wheel Arrangement: C-C

Engine: 16-710G

Output: 3,800 horsepower

Tractive Effort: various depending on gearing and wheel size

Max. Operating Speed: various depending on gearing and wheel size

Weight: 390,000 lbs.

Overall Length: 71 ft. 2 in.

crew districts. Initially, Western roads adopted the safety cab to provide a safer and more comfortable working environment, but within a few years the safety cab was standard equipment. Only Norfolk Southern and Illinois Central clung to the older cab design.

EMD's SD60M was the first model sold to US freight railroads with the advanced safety cab. The early variation was an adaption of Canadian models and featured a squared-off cab profile with three front windshields. A few years later, EMD introduced a revised cab that featured a tapered nose section and just two windshields. Another variation used the WhisperCab design (also called isolated cab) that offered better soundproofing. The SD60Is uses this cab and is distinguished from SD60Ms by the visible separation in the metal between the cab and locomotive nose. Conrail was a primary buyer of this type, opting to assemble locomotives from kits at its company shops in Altoona, Pennsylvania.

Production of the four-motor model GP60 began a year after the SD60 and spanned nine years. This high-horsepower four-axle model was aimed at fast intermodal applications and mostly was bought by Southern Pacific and Santa Fe. In addition to standard conventional cab versions, Santa Fe ordered two specialized GP60 variations: the GP60M that featured the safety cab and the cab-less GP60B B-unit. Both types were delivered in its classic warbonnet Super Fleet paint. Similar to the GP60 was the GP59s, powered by a fuel-efficient 12-cylinder 710G engine rated at 3,000 horsepower, which only Norfolk Southern bought.

Santa Fe GP60M 144 seen crossing the Mojave Desert west of Bagdad, California.
Brian Solomon

SD70MAC

EMD's SD70MAC was the first mass-produced heavy-haul diesel in North America to use a modern three-phase propulsion system. This model was introduced with great fanfare in late 1993, being heralded as the most important locomotive innovation since diesel replaced steam. Its development was made possible by a significant commitment by Burlington Northern and was based on successful testing with EMD's SD60MAC AC-traction prototypes.

A 16-710G3C engine powers the SD70MAC, but what makes it special is the Siemens-designed inverter propulsion system. Two inverters power six three-phase asynchronous traction motors, which can deliver enormous tractive effort at very slow speeds and can dramatically outperform equivalent DC motors without risk of overheating. Where an SD40-2 was rated at 87,150 pounds, continuous tractive effort, an SD70MAC has a rating of 137,000 pounds. Key to SD70MAC and other modern AC-traction locomotives is greater adhesion afforded through superior motor control and advanced wheel slip control.

Burlington Northern initially ordered 350 SD70MACs, assigning them in three-unit sets to Powder River unit coal train service. BN successor BNSF placed repeat orders for the type, while Conrail and CSX also bought the model. It was supplanted by the low-emissions SD70ACE in 2005.

SD70MAC SPECIFICATIONS

Type: Diesel-electric road locomotive

Manufacturer: EMD

Years Built: 1993-2004

Wheel Arrangement: C-C

Engine: 16-710G3B

Output: 4,000 horsepower

Continuous Tractive Effort: 137,000 lbs. (varied depending on weight)

Weight: 415,000 to 432,000, depending on options

Overall Length: 74 ft.

BNSF SD70MAC 9644 rolls along at speed with a coal train. *Tom Kline*

SD70ACE AND SD70M-2

In its final years as a General Motors subsidiary, Electro-Motive refined its heavy-freight locomotive line to comply with increasingly strict EPA emissions standards, bringing out its AC traction SD70ACe in 2005 followed by the DC traction SD70M-2. At this time, General Motors sold EMD to the Berkshire Partners LLC–Greenbriar Equity LLC consortium. While the locomotive builder continued to be known as EMD, it no longer inferred the Electro-Motive Division; instead, the name was changed to Electro-Motive Diesel. Under new ownership, the manufacturer continued to offer its SD70M-2/SD70ACe models. Five years later, in 2010, EMD was sold to Caterpillar subsidiary Progress Rail Services.

EMD's SD70M-2 and SD70ACe were essentially updated versions of its successful SD70M and SD70MAC locomotives that had been redesigned to meet the latest emissions requirements that went into effect on January 1, 2005, and they continued as the builder's primary North American heavy-freight locomotives for the better part of the following decade.

The prototype SD70ACe dated from 2003. In addition, Electro-Motive built twenty preproduction units painted for host railroads. The SD70ACe was powered by the EPA Tier 2-compliant 16-710G3C-T2 engine, rated at 4,300 horsepower. Standard features included the Electro-Motive's HTCR radial truck and the latest cab style

SD70ACE SPECIFICATIONS

Type: Diesel-electric road-freight

Manufacturer: Electro-Motive Diesel

Years Built: 2005–present

Wheel Arrangement: C-C

Engine: 16-710G3C-T2

Output: 4,300 horsepower

Tractive Effort: 155,000 pounds (continuous)

Max. Operating Speed: 65 miles per hour

Weight: 408,000-428,000 lbs. (depending on options)

Overall Length: 74 ft. 3 in.

Norfolk Southern's SD70ACe 1065, the Savanna & Atlantic heritage unit, leads a westward autorack train on the former Pennsylvania Railroad at Harrisburg, Pennsylvania, in June 2015.
Brian Solomon

Two Arkansas & Missouri SD70ACes are seen at Avoca, Arkansas, in October 2013. *Tom Kline*

redesigned to accommodate a GE-style nose door to simplify the railroad's part supply. This had been earlier applied to some late-build Union Pacific SD90MAC-Hs and exhibited a more angular appearance than EMD's standard *M*-style safety cab, used on most of its road locomotives since 1990.

The new cab and enlarged radiator intake vents externally distinguish the SD70ACE/SD70M-2 from earlier models. While the internal differences between the SD70ACe and the SD70MAC are crucial to their performance, these are invisible to the eye, as are key improvements, such as reduction in the number of inverter components on the SD70ACe. To reduce emissions and improve reliability, peak firing pressure was reduced by 15 percent on the 710 engine. This lowered stress and fatigue on primary engine components.

A variation of SD70ACe is the specialized SD70ACeP4, comparable to GE's ES44C4, a four-motor six-axle type designed to lower costs; instead of the A1A-A1A wheel arrangement used by GE, EMD's SD70ACeP4 uses the unusual B1-1B arrangement. As with GE's model, BNSF has been the primary customer.

BNSF, CSX, CN, KCS, and UP were significant buyers of the SD70ACe. In addition, small fleets were sold to Arkansas & Missouri, Montana Rail Link, and Quebec North Shore & Labrador, plus lines in Mexico and Australia. Canadian National and Norfolk Southern bought most of the SD70M-2s.

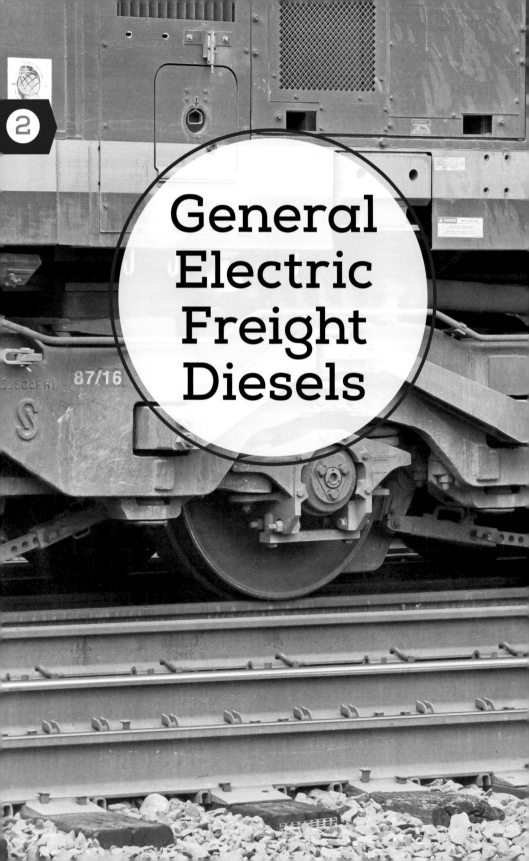

General Electric Freight Diesels

GENERAL ELECTRIC
DASH 8

In the 1980s, General Electric's Dash 8 line introduced onboard microprocessor controls to its locomotive design in order to improve fuel efficiency, locomotive component reliability, and performance. Yet, externally, the Dash 8 was distinguished from GE's early models by its powerful boxy appearance. GE introduced the Dash 8 with experimental prototypes, followed by small fleets of preproduction prototype models that served as functional test beds. These worked in regular revenue service and were painted and lettered for the railroads they served. GE called them "Classics," and are identified externally by their contoured cab profile and humpback dynamic brake grid housings. Among the advantages of the Dash 8 line was a powerful traction alternator/rectifier capable of supplying high voltage and high current to motors without the need for electrical transition, as was common on GE's earlier locomotive types.

In 1987 and 1988, GE offered what it called the Enhanced Dash 8, a high-horsepower, four-motor

EXAMPLE OF GENERAL ELECTRIC DASH 8; DASH 8-40CW

Type: road freight locomotive

Manufacturer: General Electric

Years Built: 1989-1994

Wheel Arrangement: C-C

Engine: GE 7FDL16

Output: 4,000 horsepower

Tractive Effort: 108,900 lbs. at 11 mph

Max. Operating Speed: 70 mph

Weight: 390,000 lbs.

Overall Length: 70 ft. 8 in.

In March 1989, New York Susquehanna & Western DASH 8-40B 4002 leads a double-stack train at West Middlebury, New York. *Brian Solomon*

OPPOSITE: GE offered its six-motor steerable truck as an option. *Brian Solomon*

model B39-8 that featured a boxy cab. Mass production of its Dash 8 line began in 1987 with two models: the four-motor Dash 8-40B for intermodal service, and the six-motor Dash 8-40C for heavy road freight. As inferred by the "40" in their designation, both were rated at 4,000 horsepower. GE built 581 Dash 8-40Cs, selling them to Chicago & North Western, Conrail, CSX, and Union Pacific. CN now operates a fleet of former UP units.

GE began offering the new North American safety cab as an option for its Dash 8 locomotives from 1989 to 1990. Within a few years, nearly all American railroads adopted this wide-nose cab style for road locomotives. Santa Fe, Amtrak, and Caltrans acquired four-axle Dash 8s with the safety cab (models Dash 8-40BW and Dash 8-32BWH), while the majority of safety cab Dash 8 locomotives were 4,000-horsepower, heavy-haul, six-motor models as typified by the Dash 8-40CW. A few late-build units were uprated, and their higher horsepower rating is reflected in their model designation: Santa Fe and Union Pacific ordered Dash 8-41CWs, while CSX received Dash 8-44CWs. A Canadian variation was a six-axle unit with a full-width car body and the four-window Canadian wide-nose cab. Domestic Dash 8 production was phased out with the introduction of the Dash 9 line in 1994.

A pair of new LMX B39-8s work east on the old Chicago, Burlington & Quincy at Zearing, Illinois.
Brian Solomon

GENERAL ELECTRIC
DASH 9 AND AC4400CW

General Electric's Dash 9 line was a marketing tool intended to demonstrate technological improvements to its standard freight locomotive line, but it still shared many common features with late-production Dash 8 locomotives. Dash 9s are similar in appearance to late-production Dash 8s, but with safety cabs, minor external differences in the step and hand-rail arrangements, slightly thicker radiator wings, and the first application of the distinctive-looking HiAd (high-adhesion truck) that visually distinguished Dash 9s from Dash 8 models. Internally, improvements such as electronic fuel injection and split cooling, which had been recently offered as options on late-era Dash 8s, were offered as standard Dash 9 equipment.

Model Dash 9-44CW was by far the most popular for purchase. Norfolk Southern didn't embrace the North American safety cab and bought a fleet of Dash 9-40Cs with conventional cabs; however, its later Dash 9-40CWs featured safety cabs. Both models were rated at 4,000 horsepower rather than 4,400 horsepower, to lower fuel consumption in the highest throttle position.

EXAMPLE OF GENERAL ELECTRIC DASH 9: DASH 9-40C

Type: road freight locomotive

Years Built: 1995

Manufacturer: General Electric

Wheel Arrangement: C-C

Engine: GE 7FDL16

Output: 4,000 horsepower

Tractive Effort: NA

Max. Operating Speed: NA

Weight: 410,000 lbs.

Overall Length: 73 ft. 2 in.

A trio of Norfolk Southern DASH 9 lead westward symbol intermodal freight 21M at Gallitzin, Pennsylvania. *Brian Solomon*

GE's AC4400CW, introduced about the same time, is also similar in appearance to the Dash 9. However, the GE uses a fundamentally different traction system and is GE's first commercial alternating-current traction locomotive, equivalent to EMD's SD70MAC. Modern three-phase AC traction uses computer-controlled high-voltage electronics to produce current for traction motors. This addition of computer electronics permitted an increase in tractive power while improving dynamic braking and significantly lowering the life-cycle costs of major electrical components.

CSX's 500 Series AC4400CWs, known as *heavies*, were a variation on the basic design. These locomotives have greater tractive effort as a result of having an extra 10 tons of ballast, which make them more effective in slow-speed mineral service on steep grades. GE offered its steerable trucks as an option to reduce wheel and rail wear. This truck style has remained a customer option on other modern diesels, including Evolution Series units.

Visually, the AC4400CW may be distinguished from comparable DC Models by the large box behind the cab on the left side of the locomotive that houses high-voltage inverters. When GE's Evolution Series entered regular production in late 2004, it ended domestic production of Dash 9 and AC4400CW lines.

Kansas City Southern AC4400CW 4596 crosses the Colorado River at Wharton, Texas, on April 30, 2014. *Tom Kline*

GE AC6000CW

In the mid-1990s, large fleets of 3,000-horsepower locomotives were approaching retirement age, and GE anticipated a market for 6,000-horsepower locomotives that would have allowed railroads to replace older 3,000-horsepower units on a two-for-one basis. It introduced the AC6000CW beginning in 1995, powered by its new GE 7HDL engine jointly designed by GE and German engine manufacturer Duetz MWM, specifically to meet the greater power demands. Earlier locomotives in this horsepower range had used twin prime movers.

Greater power required more space and greater cooling capacity, and the AC6000CW required a larger car body with noticeably larger radiators housed in larger "wings" at the rear of the locomotive.

CSX and Union Pacific were the only buyers. In UP's case, it was pressed for power and couldn't wait for the new 7HDL, so during the mid-1990s, it ordered a "convertible" variation that resembled true AC6000CWs (featuring the large body) but which was powered by the standard 7FDL engine rated at 4,400 horsepower. (Union Pacific, which has tended not to adopt GE's modern model designations, classified these locomotives as C44/60AC.) These were intended to eventually be converted to 6,000-horsepower locomotives.

The AC6000CW was envisioned as an intermodal-service locomotive, yet in practice AC6000CWs have largely worked heavy carload trains. The vision of 6,000-horsepower units replacing pairs of GP40/SD40 types failed to materialize, and these big locomotives have become curiosities when compared with the large fleets of 4,400-horsepower GE Safety Cab models. Reliability is a greater consideration than total output in modern railroading, and CSX's dissatisfaction with the 6,000-horsepower HDL engine has led to replacing engines on some of its AC6000CW locomotives with GE's more successful 4,400-horsepower GEVO diesel.

AC6000CW SPECIFICATIONS

Type: Diesel-electric road-freight

Manufacturer: General Electric

Years Built: Beginning in 1995

Wheel Arrangement: C-C

Engine: GE 7HDL16

Output: 6,000 horsepower

Tractive Effort: 166,000 lbs. (continuous)

Max. Operating Speed: NA

Weight: 420,000 lbs.

Overall Length: 76 ft.

On June 19, 2015, symbol freight Q423 is westbound at Worcester, Massachusetts, led by CSX AC6000CW 693, powered by a model HDL 6,000 hp diesel. *Brian Solomon*

EVOLUTION SERIES

GE's development of its Evolution Series diesels was driven by the need to comply with more stringent EPA-mandated Tier 2 engine emissions requirements that went into effect in 2005. Anticipating this change, GE engineered a new low-emissions diesel engine, called the GEVO, which is key to its Evolution Series models.

GE offered the Evolution with either AC or DC traction systems, represented as models ES44AC and ES44DC, respectively. Despite the significantly different electrical systems, these two basic models appear nearly the same externally and shared a family resemblance with Dash 9 and AC4400CW models. Key to distinguishing the Evolution models from earlier GE Safety Cab locomotives is the substantially thicker radiator wings at the back of the engine.

Initially, six-axle six-motor models were the standard types, however, GE introduced its ES44C4, an unusual AC traction model that uses a variation of the A1A truck. The center axle is unpowered, essentially making these six-axle four-motor models, but with an unusual feature that, when starting the weight distribution, can be shifted away from the center axle to allow for greater adhesive force on the powered axles. The intent of this type was to provide performance characteristics similar to a DC traction Evolution locomotive without the high price tag associated with a heavy-haul six-motor AC type. BNSF Railway was the initial customer, but other railroads have since bought C4s.

Not all railroads have adopted GE's model designations for their classification systems, and this can lead to confusion as to the correct way to refer to various locomotive models. There are valid reasons why railroads may classify locomotives differently. A company may wish to distinguish between locomotives of the same model type that have distinct operating characteristics. For example, GE model designations do not indicate locomotive weight, but CSX ordered locomotives weighing 432,000 pounds (total serviced locomotive weight), which is higher than normal for AC4400s and ES44ACs. To distinguish these heavier ES44ACs, CSX classified them as ES44AH—*H* for heavy—and this is

ES44DC SPECIFICATIONS

Type: Diesel-electric road-freight

Manufacturer: General Electric

Years Built: 2004

Wheel Arrangement: C-C

Engine: 12-GEVO

Output: 4,390 horsepower

Tractive Effort: 105,680 lbs. (continuous)

Max. Operating Speed: 75 mph with 83:20 gearing

Weight: 420,000 lbs.

Overall Length: 73 ft. 2 in.

printed on the side of the locomotives. In a similar manner, Union Pacific classifies its heavy ES44ACs as C45AH. Both are correct: one is the GE builder's model and the other is the railroad's internal classification.

Brand-new Florida East Coast General Electric ES44C4s 801 and 809 lead an intermodal train.
Walter E. Zullig

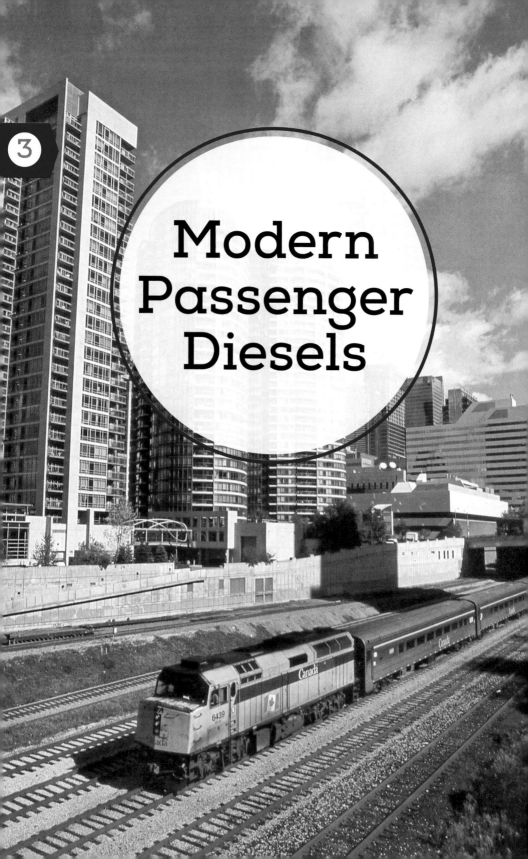

Modern Passenger Diesels

EMD F40PH

In 1976, EMD adapted its F40PH model for Amtrak, basing the guts on its successful GP40-2 road-switcher freight locomotive. The boxy F40PH was the face of Amtrak for the next two decades, handling the majority of its trains outside of electric territory in the Northeast. The F40PH is a cowl type, with a non-structural sheet metal body covering similar to that used by EMD's six-motor FP45 and SDP40F models. It required a modified electrical system for head-end power; on the early F40PHs the prime mover supplied head end power (HEP).

Amtrak initially ordered F40PHs to power corridor services hauling the new Budd-built HEP-equipped Amfleet cars, while long-distance services were to be handled by new EMD SDP40Fs. When the SDP40Fs unexpectedly developed problems Amtrak opted to order more F40PHs, so between 1976 and 1987 they took delivery of 210 units (numbers 200 to 409). Some of these were technically considered model F40PHRs because in theory they incorporated components recycled from traded SDP40Fs.

A variety of suburban passenger operators also bought F40 models, beginning with Chicago's Regional Transportation Authority (the oversight body for Metra). Metra went on to order the F40PH-2 and uniquely designed F40PHM-2. The latter type is distinguished by its unusual cab profile that reaches forward to directly intersect the nose section. In 1985, the State of California

F40PH SPECIFICATIONS

Type: Road passenger diesel

Manufacturer: EMD

Years Built: 1976-1988

Wheel Arrangement: B-B

Engine: 16-645E

Output: 3,000 horsepower

Tractive Effort: Depends on gear ratio and options

Max. Operating Speed: 103 mph with 57:20 gearing

Weight: 259,000 lbs.

Overall Length: 56 ft. 2 in.

OPPOSITE: VIA Rail F40PH-2D 6439 approaches Spadina Avenue in Toronto. *Brian Solomon*

BELOW: VIA Rail F40PH-2D 6407 is heading west from Montreal, Quebec, on October 23, 2004. The F40PH-2D was a variation on the basic F40PH only sold in Canada. *Brian Solomon*

bought eighteen F40PH-2s for the San Francisco Peninsula "Commutes" (not "commuter"), which were unusual because of their late use of the classic Southern Pacific-style headlights, with both fixed and a red oscillating light. Massachusetts Bay Transportation Authority was another early F40PH user. In 1987 and 1988, it augmented its original fleet with the improved F40PH-2C models that features an auxiliary Cummins diesel engine and separate generator for HEP. This model is just over 8 feet longer than original F40PHs.

In the 1990s, MK Rail/Motive Power Industries' Boise Locomotive constructed F40PH-3Cs using an adaptation of EMD's F40PH type. These use most of the same fundamental components of the EMD-built locomotives and cosmetically appear very similar to the classic EMD-build F40PH. Like the F40PH-2, these use an auxiliary engine to produce three-phase AC head end-power. The prime mover is rated at 3,200 horsepower compared with the F40PH's 3,000. Among the operators for this relatively unusual type is California's Altamont Commuter Express that operates between Stockton and San Jose via its namesake pass.

Chicago Metra F40PHM-2 211 featuring the unusual cab profile provides a contrast with 177, which is an ordinary F40PH-2. *Brian Solomon*

MOTIVEPOWER INDUSTRIES
HSP-46

One of the most modern passenger locomotives in the United States is the HSP-46, a cooperative venture between MotivePower Industries and General Electric. MPI assembles the locomotives using primary components developed for GE's Evolution-Series freight locomotives, including an EPA Tier-3 compliant 12-cylinder GEVO diesel, and state of the art three-phase AC traction system. Head-end power (HEP) is provided from a static inverter. The locomotive's distinctive shape is the work of Cesar Vergara, the industrial designer whose prolific career has included the design of GE's GENESIS™ diesel body as well as Amtrak's original GENESIS™ paint livery, which featured an unusual arrangement of fading stripes toward the back of the locomotive.

Boston-based Massachusetts Bay Transportation Authority ordered 20 of this new type in 2010, and later upped this to 40 units. The first of these new locomotives entered service in 2014. They are assigned to push-pull commuter services from both North and South Stations, working former Boston & Albany, Boston & Maine, and New Haven Railroad routes. These are painted in a modern adaption of the MBTA purple, yellow and silver livery, which in MBTA tradition features large road numbers on the roof.

MOTIVEPOWER INDUSTRIES HSP-46 SPECIFICATIONS

Type: B-B, diesel-electric passenger locomotive

Manufacturer: MotivePower Industries

Years Built: 2013–present

Wheel Arrangement: B-B

Engine: GE 12GEVO

Output: 4,650 horsepower

Tractive Effort: Starting 65,200 lbs. at 9 mph

Max. Operating Speed: 110 mph (with 74:29 gearing)

Weight: 287,500 lbs.

Overall Length: 71 ft.

MBTA's HSP-46 2026 arrives at Worcester Union Station with a train from Boston on July 6, 2015.
Brian Solomon

F59PHI

In the mid-1990s, California's strict locomotive emissions standards, combined with a popular mandate for state-funded Amtrak services corridor services, encouraged EMD to work with the state in the development of a true passenger locomotive. Using the road-switcher format F59PH (covered previously), EMD transformed it into a modern streamlined passenger diesel that met California's emissions and styling requirements. This was designated model F59PHI. (The "I" indicates use of EMD's isolated WhisperCab™.) Although it has a distinctive appearance, this locomotive shares a cowl structure with the F40PH, FP45, and some Canadian freight models, but with a more aerodynamic design to reduce wind resistance. The front features a fiberglass composite nose backed by thick steel plates to help protect the locomotive crew in event of an accident. The F59PHI's pleasing, streamlined appearance contrasts with common utilitarian locomotives that had ruled North American railroads during the previous four decades. In addition to California's acquisition, a variety of other passenger service operators ordered the F59PHI for suburban and intermediate length runs.

While the F59PHI has a very different appearance from F59PH, the two locomotives share primary components, including the 12-cylinder 710G3 diesel and electrical system. An auxiliary engine and alternator supply head-end power for passenger cars. Although the F59PHI was built in relatively small numbers, the core equipment used in this locomotive was also adapted for Irish Rail's Class 201 (Electro-Motive model JT42HCW), a dual-service, six-motor, double-cab diesel built for 5-foot 3-inch gauge tracks, while a similar locomotive, Model JT42CWR (known in the UK as the Class 66), has been exported to a variety of standard-gauge freight operators in Europe.

F59PHI SPECIFICATIONS

Type: Road passenger diesel

Manufacturer: EMD/General Motors Locomotive Group

Years Built: Beginning 1994

Wheel Arrangement: B-B

Engine: 12-710G

Output: 3,200 horsepower

Tractive Effort: NA

Max. Operating Speed: 110 mph with 56:21 gearing

Weight: 270,000 lbs.

Overall Length: 58 ft. 7 in.

On June 5, 2008, Metrolink F59PHI basks in the bold California sun at Los Angeles Union Station. *Brian Solomon*

Long Island Rail Road DM30AC 509 leads a double-deck commuter train at Jamaica, Queens.
Patrick Yough

EMD DE30AC

Unique to New York's Long Island Rail Road are two similar and unusual looking Electro-Motive Division locomotive models. LIRR bought forty-six new locomotives in the late 1990s, twenty-three each of models DM30AC and DE30AC for push-pull suburban services. Both types are powered by 12-cylinder EMD 710G3B diesels rated at 3,000 horsepower. The DM30AC (LIRR numbers 500 to 522) is a specialized hybrid dual mode type, similar in concept to EMD's FL9 and General Electric's P23AC-DM. These are designed to draw current from line-side high-voltage direct current third rail in New York-area electrified territory, or take power from its onboard diesel. Working from the third rail it can draw up to 4,000 amps continuously. By contrast, the DE30AC is strictly a diesel-electric (LIRR numbers 400 to 422). Both types feature a low-profile monocoque body (where the chassis is integral to the body) to accommodate restrictive clearances in New York tunnels. Locomotive sides are stainless steel. Although an Electro-Motive design, these locomotives were assembled by Super Steel Products of Schenectady, New York.

DM30AC SPECIFICATIONS

Type: Dual-mode passenger diesel-electric/electric

Manufacturer: EMD/General Motors Locomotive Group

Years Built: 1998

Wheel Arrangement: B-B

Engine: EMD 12N-710G3B-EC

Output: 3,000 horsepower

Tractive Effort: NA

Max. Operating Speed: 100 mph

Weight: 294,000 lbs.

Overall Length: 75 ft.

Height: 14 ft. 3.5 in.

GENERAL ELECTRIC
GENESIS™

Since the mid-1990s, North American long-distance passenger services have been characterized by General Electric's GENESIS™ diesels. Unlike most North American passenger locomotives built from 1960s to the early 1990s, it is an all-new, long-distance locomotive designed specifically for passenger service, blending European-style monocoque body with American diesel-electric technology tuned for fast passenger train service; it rides on fabricated bolster-less high-speed trucks, while its shape and size complies with New York City terminal trackage restrictive clearances.

Unlike cowl-type locomotives, such as the F40 models that use a non-structural sheet metal covering, the GENESIS™ monocoque body shell is integral to the locomotive structure. It was styled by industrial designer Cesar Vergara, whose vision emphasizes angular shapes with flat surfaces.

GE built three GENESIS™ models. Though these appear nearly identical because all use the same body shell, they have significant internal differences. The GENESIS™ Series 1 was the original model, designated by GE as Dash 8-40BP

GENESIS EXAMPLE: P32AC-DM

Type: dual-mode diesel-electric/electric passenger locomotive

Years Built: beginning 1995

Manufacturer: General Electric

Wheel Arrangement: B-B

Engine: GE 7FDL12

Output: 3,200 horsepower

Tractive Effort: 38,500 lbs. (continuous)

Max. Operating Speed: 110 mph with 74:29 gearing

Weight: 277,000 lbs.

Overall Length: 69 ft.

(and known by Amtrak as the P40). This was adapted from GE's Dash 8 freight locomotive, and employs 1980s-era electrical technology including GE's 16-cylinder 7FDL diesel rated at 4,000 horsepower. GE built forty-four for Amtrak during 1993 and 1994 (numbered in the 800-series). Originally, these featured an unusual paint scheme with red and blue stripes that appeared to fade toward the back of the locomotives. As of 2015, only a few remained active on Amtrak; some locomotives were conveyed to Connecticut's Shore Line East, and others to NJ Transit.

The most common GENESIS™ is GE's 4,250 horsepower P42DC (common known as the P42). This is based on the more advanced GE Dash 9 technology and features Electronic Fuel Injection and a more modern braking controls. Amtrak bought most of these beginning in 1996, which are numbered from 1 to 207, while Canada's VIA Rail received twenty-one units in 2001 (numbers 900 to 920) that are geared for 100 miles per hour operation.

The third variety is by far the most unusual: this is a dual-mode version, model P32AC-DM. It is alternatively a diesel-electric and straight electric, and can change from one mode to the other at speed. Working as an electric it uses third-rail shoes to draw current from line-side third rail on New York City electrified lines. Amtrak bought P32AC-DMs equipped with overrunning third-rail shoes for its Empire Corridor service from Penn Station, while Metro-North and Connecticut DOT acquired similar locomotives but with under-running shoes to work into Grand Central Terminal. Both types replaced aging former New Haven Railroad dual mode FL9s (see page 187). While similar in appearance to the other GENESIS™ models, the P32AC-DM involves other notable differences: instead of the 16-cylinder engine with traditional DC traction it has a 12-cylinder 7FDL engine, and a three-phase AC traction system.

ABOVE LEFT: At Ashland, Virginia, on June 8, 2015, a pair of DASH 8-40BPs (GENESIS™ Series 1) lead Amtrak's northward Autotrain, train 53. *Brian Solomon*

ABOVE RIGHT: CDOT P32AC-DMs 229 is seen at Stamford, Connecticut, with a Danbury-branch train. *Walter E. Zullig*

OPPOSITE: Amtrak GE P42DC 42 is uniquely painted to honor America's Veterans. *Brian Solomon*

MOTIVE POWER INDUSTRIES
MPXPRESS™

MotivePower Industries's four MPXpress™ models were among the most common passenger diesels purchased by North American commuter railroads in the 2000s. These models use a futuristic streamlined locomotive cab design that looks like something you'd expect to find on a Mars lander, plus EMD-designed primary components, including diesel engines, main electrical parts, and Blomberg B style trucks.

In 2003, Caltrain (which operates San Francisco—San Jose—Gilroy services) was the first to acquire MPI's MPXpress™ commuter locomotives, with an order for six model MP36PH-3Cs. These were ostensibly bought for service expansion in the form of the "Baby Bullet" limited expresses operated with new Bombardier bi-levels acquired at the same time. The MP36PH-3C model has become the most common member of the MPXpress™ family. This is a 3,600 horsepower locomotive that produces head-end power (HEP) using an auxiliary diesel and separate generator. Other MP36PH-3C operators in the United States include Salt Lake City's Front Runner, Los Angeles-area Metrolink, Massachusetts Bay Transportation Authority

MP40PH-3C SPECIFICATIONS

Type: B-B, diesel-electric passenger locomotive

Manufacturer: MotivePower Industries

Years Built: Beginning 2003

Wheel Arrangement: B-B

Engine: EMD 16-710G3B-T2

Output: 4,000 horsepower

Tractive Effort: NA

Max. Operating Speed: 93 mph (depending on gearing)

Weight: 295,500 lbs.

Overall Length: 68 ft.

(which acquired a pair of surplus Front Runner units in 2011), Maryland's MARC, Minneapolis-area Northstar, New Mexico Rail Runner Express, and Washington D.C.-based Virginia Railway Express. British Columbia's West Coast Express acquired a lone MP36PH-3C, giving it the smallest fleet of MPXpress™ locomotives.

In 2009, Toronto-based GO Transit was first to acquire the more powerful MP40PH-3C model, powered by a modern low-emission variation of EMD's 16-710G (rated at 4,000 horsepower) instead of variations of the 16-645F diesel found in the 3,600 horsepower models. Seattle's Sounder also acquired a small MP40PH-3C fleet.

Orlando-based Sunrail ordered a fleet of eight refurbished locomotives based on the core of old EMD GP40s that had been previously rebuilt for Maryland MARC. These are MP36PH-Qs and incorporate elements of the MPXpress™ design, including the streamlined cab; but instead of a fully enclosed car body, it features a hood style road-switcher rear body. These were the most recent members of the MPXpress™ family, built between 2013-2014 for the Florida start-up service.

Florida's Sunrail began operations in 2014 with a fleet of eight Motive Power Industries MPXpress™ model MP36PH-Q locomotives, such as 102, pictured at the old Atlantic Coast Line station in Orlando. *Walter E. Zullig*

OPPOSITE: On June 12, 2010, GO Transit MP40PH-3C, working at the back of a push-pull set, passes beneath the Bathurst Street Bridge as it accelerates away from Toronto Union Station. *Brian Solomon*

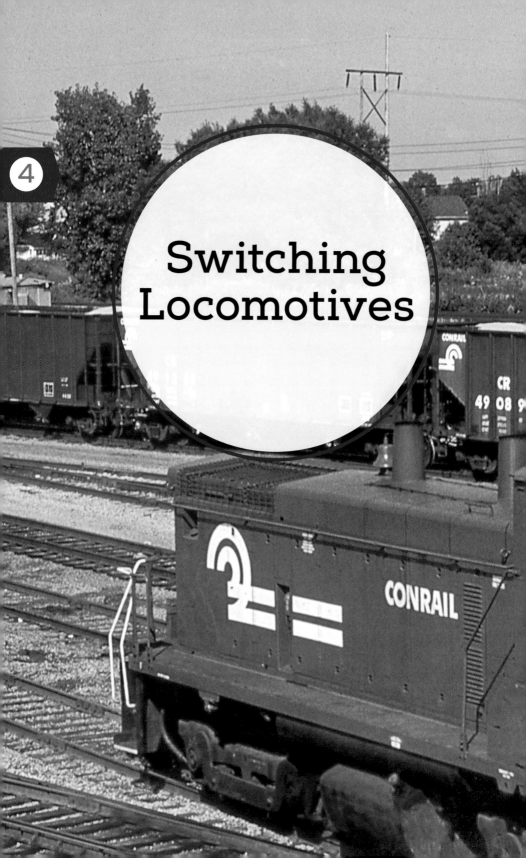

4

Switching Locomotives

EMD SW1000/ SW1500

Introduction of EMD 645E series engines in the mid-1960s allowed EMD to offer a more powerful standard switcher. Its SW1500 was a 1,500-horsepower switcher model built from 1966 to 1974 powered by a 12-cylinder 645 non-turbocharged engine, which effectively supplanted the SW1200 in EMD's locomotive catalog. The type was slightly larger than earlier models and can be easily distinguished by its boxy cab. Many American railroads bought SW1500s; however, during the period of its production the market for diesel switchers declined dramatically as railroads shifted freight traffic toward intermodal and unit train operations that favored end-to-end operations. Also, most railroads discontinued traditional passenger services that had once required switching of consists at terminal. By contrast, modern commuter train arrangements came to favor fixed push-pull consists that rarely required switching. The SW1500 was more than just a slow-speed yard switcher, and several railroads routinely assigned SW1500s in multiple to road freight service. Similar in appearance was EMD's SW1000, which primarily differed in its diesel engine prime mover, which was an 8-cylinder 645E rated at 1,000 horsepower. The external difference was the use of a single stack on the SW1500 instead of two. Model variation SW1001 featured a low-clearance cab and was sold in greater numbers than SW1000.

EMD SW1500 SPECIFICATIONS

Type: Diesel-electric switcher

Manufacturer: EMD

Years Built: 1966-1974

Wheel Arrangement: B-B

Engine: EMD 12-645E (aspirated with a Roots blower)

Output: 1,500 horsepower

Tractive Effort: 45,000 lbs. at 12 mph

Max. Operating Speed: 65 mph

Weight: 260,000 lbs.

Overall Length: 44 ft. 8 in.

OPPOSITE: Conrail SW1500 9578 works at Buffalo, New York, in September 1989. *Brian Solomon*

BELOW: Denver & Rio Grande Western SW1000 144 was a relic by the time of this September 1998 photograph at Denver's North Yard. *Brian Solomon*

EMD MP15

EMD's MP15 model designation (sometimes listed as MP15DC) inferred "Multi Purpose" and implied that these locomotives were more versatile than the switcher models they superseded. The early MP15 models were similar in appearance and application to the SW1500, except that they were slightly longer and rode on the Blomberg B truck instead of either the AAR-style truck or EMD's two-axle Flexi-Coil truck.

Like the SW1500, these locomotives were powered by a 12-645E (an engine aspirated with a Roots blower rather than a turbocharger). From 1975 on, an advanced variation was offered, designated MP15AC, that featured a Dash 2 style electrical system using modular electronics in place of conventional relays and an alternator-rectifier. It also used a modified air-flow system with air-intake vents located on the forward portion of the long-hood. This locomotive was 18 inches longer than the MP15DC type. The MP15AC's "AC" designation does not infer application of three-phase propulsion—an advanced system innovated two decades later and introduced on the SD70MAC (see page 21). The MP15T was a late-era variation introduced in the 1980s; notably, this involved a further modified body style and significantly was powered by a turbocharged 8-cylinder 645E3 diesel—thus the "T" in the designation.

EMD MP15DC SPECIFICATIONS

Type: Diesel-electric switcher

Manufacturer: EMD

Years Built: 1974-1980

Wheel Arrangement: B-B

Engine: EMD 12-645E (aspirated with a Roots blower)

Output: 1,500 horsepower

Tractive Effort: NA

Max. Operating Speed: 65 mph

Weight: 258,000 lbs.

Overall Length: 47 ft. 8 in./48 ft. 8 in. (depending on build date)

Genesee & Wyoming MP15 number 45 works cab-first as it crosses the former New York Central System Peanut Line at P&L Junction in Caledonia, New York. *Brian Solomon*

Former Santa Fe CF7 2427 is an example of one of the converted F-units featuring a fabricated "Topeka Cab." *Dan Howard*

SANTA FE CF7

During the 1970s, Santa Fe undertook an extensive F-unit conversion that transformed the 233 traditional car-body style units F3A, F7A, and F9A into road-switcher style locomotives. They designated these as CF7, with the letter C, standing for "converted." Santa Fe remanufactured the locomotives at its company shops in Cleburne, Texas. Rebuilding retained and incorporated the F's primary mechanical and electric components, including the 567 diesel, Blomberg B trucks, control stand (throttle and air brake controls), and fuel tanks. Originally, 179 of the CF7 conversions retained a portion of the car body and cab windows that hinted at the locomotive's F-unit lineage. Later conversions dispensed entirely with the car body and instead featured the fabricated "Topeka cab." This had many benefits, and later, additional CF7s were retrofitted.

A road switcher has a fundamentally different structure than a car body-type locomotive, so Santa Fe needed to fabricate a platform frame and built a sheet-metal hood to replace the F's structural truss car body. This required relocating the radiators and radiator fans to far ends of the long hood (emulating the arrangement on Electro-Motive's road switchers). The converted locomotives were all rated at 1,500 horsepower with 62:15 gearing.

CF7 SPECIFICATIONS

Type: Converted diesel-electric road switcher

Years Rebuilt: 1970-1978

Manufacturer: Santa Fe Cleburne shops with EMD components

Wheel Arrangement: B-B

Engine: EMD 16-567BC

Output: 1,500 horsepower

Max. Operating Speed: 65 mph

Weight: 249,000 lbs.

Overall Length: 52 ft.

ABOVE: Pioneer Valley Railroad CF7s 2597 and 2558 catch the sun at the railroad's Westfield, Massachusetts yard. *Brian Solomon*

BELOW: Former Santa Fe CF7s have ended up on short line railroads across the United States, including the Louisiana & Delta. *Brian Solomon*

Between 1984 and 1988, Santa Fe sold many CF7s to short lines, and as a result the model that was unique to Santa Fe has, during the last thirty years, worked on more than fifty different railroads. One of the largest post-Santa Fe fleets was Amtrak's twenty-five units, which were assigned to work-train (maintenance train) service and as yard switchers but rarely to haul passenger trains.

MK RAIL/MOTIVEPOWER INDUSTRIES
SWITCHERS

MK Rail was a predecessor to today's MotivePower Industries. During the early 1990s it developed an experimental, low-horsepower, low-emissions switcher powered by a Caterpillar G3516 engine and fueled with liquefied natural gas (LNG). It built just four: two each for Santa Fe and Union Pacific. These were assigned to yard duties in the Los Angeles area, where engine emissions are a sensitive issue. Later, Santa Fe successor BNSF acquired the two UP units, putting the entire production run of this rare type under common operation.

During its transition from MK Rail to MotivePower Industries, the locomotive builder offered a diesel switcher, model MK1500D, which looked similar to LNG units but was a common diesel-electric. The locomotives utilized the frames of older units, typically EMD GP7s and GP9s, and used a variety of EMD components, including Blomberg trucks and General Motors D78B nose-suspended traction motors. The model designation on late-build units was changed to MP1500D. Port Terminal Railway Association operated the largest roster of MK1500D/ MP1500D locomotives that have worked industrial trackage in the Houston, Texas, area since they were delivered in 1996.

MK1500D/ MP1500D SPECIFICATIONS

Type: Diesel-electric road switcher

Manufacturer: MK Rail/ MotiverPower Industries

Dates Built: 1996-1999

Wheel Arrangement: B-B

Engine: Caterpillar 3512A

Output: 1,400 horsepower

Tractive Effort: NA

Max. Operating Speed: 70 mph

Weight: 256,000 lbs.

Overall Length: 56 ft. 2 in.

Port Terminal Railway Association near Houston, Texas, has a large fleet of MK1500D switchers. Note that the MK1500D rides on an EMD Blomberg B truck.
Tom Kline

Pictured at Mykawa, Texas, is a BNSF National Railway Equipment model 3GS-21B rated at 2,100 horsepower. *Tom Kline*

NATIONAL RAILWAY EQUIPMENT GENSET
LOCOMOTIVES

National Railway Equipment, based in Mt. Vernon, Illinois, is a supplier of new and remanufactured locomotives. The company developed its N-ViroMotive line of Genset locomotive models, in which each Genset power plant represents a completely self-contained diesel engine-generator combination. Instead of a single larger diesel, typical of traditional American heavy diesel locomotives, NRE Gensets are typically powered with low-emissions Cummins QSK19C diesels, intended to reduce emissions and lower fuel costs while offering superior tractive effort over conventional diesel-electric models. The locomotives take advantage of common components, such as traditional EMD nose-suspended traction motors.

NRE's switcher and road-switcher Gensets use descriptive designations: its four-axle four-motor types are the 1GS-7B, a single Genset switcher locomotive rated at 700 horsepower; the 2GS-14B, a dual-Genset road switcher rated at 1,400 horsepower; and the 3GS-21B, a triple-Genset road switcher offering 2,100 horsepower—intended to replace older EMD GP38/GP38-2 locomotives. It six-motor model, termed 3GS-21C, is a triple-Genset six-motor locomotive rated at 2,100 horsepower; it offers output approximately equivalent to an EMD SD38, and is ideal for slow speed, high-tractive effort switcher applications, such as hump yard work.

NRE 2GS-14B SPECIFICATIONS

Type: B-B, Genset road-switcher

Manufacturer: National Railway Equipment

Years Built: Beginning 2007

Wheel Arrangement: B-B

Engine: Two Cummins QSK19C

Output: 1,400 horsepower

Max. Operating Speed: 70 mph

Tractive Effort: NA

Weight: 258,000 lbs.

Overall Length: 56 ft. 2 in.

NORFOLK SOUTHERN
GP33ECO

Norfolk Southern's GP33ECO was introduced in Atlanta in 2012 and in Chicago in 2013, a response to these cities desiring to improve the air quality around rail yards. The railroad worked with the federal Congestion Mitigation and Air Quality (CMAQ) improvement program that provided funding to assist in the financing of twenty-five GP33ECO mothers and thirteen RP-M4C slugs (weighted unpowered units with extra traction motors) to be divided between the two cities. By using CMAQ funds, cities are able to seek a greater emissions reduction from the railroad than is normally required of EPA regulations of older locomotives.

A benefit for NS is that it can reduce locomotives on a two-for-one basis by using the slug-sets, and this further reduces emissions and helps lower costs. The GP33ECOs meet EPA Tier 3 emissions requirements and will replace locomotives that meet the older Tier 0 or Tier 0+ emissions standards. Chicago and Atlanta used separate funding initiatives, but both groups of locomotives were built together.

In designing the GP33ECO, Norfolk Southern worked with the core old EMD GP50 to take recycled AR-15 alternator and D-87 traction motors. During the rebuilding, the GP50s 16-cylinder 16-645F prime mover was swapped for a more modern fuel-efficient low-emissions 12-cylinder 12-710G3B-T3 engine, and the control system was replaced with EMD's EM2000 microprocessor control system. The locomotives feature a NS designed split cooling radiator system, electronic fuel injection, new CCB26 electronic air brakes, a larger 6-cylinder air compressor, along with remote control equipment and a new Admiral cab. The rebuilding took place at NS's Altoona shops in Pennsylvania.

The new locomotives are assigned the 4700 number series, and the RP-M4C slugs follow in 610 series (previously assigned to its slug fleet). NS 4700-4714s are assigned to the Chicago area while NS 4715-4724s are assigned to Georgia operations. All ten GP33ECOs for Atlanta will be mated with RP-M4C slugs while the remaining three will be assigned to Chicago. Delivery began in February 2015. *Chris Guss*

The Norfolk Southern GP33ECO is designed to work with a slug (unpowered unit with extra traction motors), and the supporting plug-in receptacles can be seen on the rear pilot.
Chris Guss

GP33ECO SPECIFICATIONS

Type: Diesel-electric road/ yard locomotive

Manufacturer: Norfolk Southern

Years Built: Beginning 2015

Wheel Arrangement: B-B

Engine: EMD 12-710G3B-Y3

Output: 3,300 horsepower

Tractive Effort: 64,200 lbs.

Max. Operating Speed: 70 mph

Weight: NA

Overall Length: 59 ft. 2 in.

Passenger Electrics

Amtrak is expected to retire the last of its AEM-7s in 2016, leaving the only examples in Philadelphia and Maryland-area suburban service. SEPTA AEM-7 2302 is westbound at Bryn Mawr, Pennsylvania.
Brian Solomon

AEM-7
ELECTRIC

In the late 1970s, Amtrak imported a Swedish State Railways (Staten Järnväger, SJ) Rc4 electric for tests. Based on the success of this experiment, a variant of the Rc electric was designed for Amtrak for high speed passenger service at 125 miles per hour. Amtrak's AEM-7 fleet was assembled by General Motors' Electro Motive Division at La Grange, Illinois, with body shells built by Budd. While Amtrak's AEM-7s resemble the Swedish prototypes, they use a stronger body to fulfill American safety standards.

Amtrak initially ordered forty- seven AEM-7s with additional AEM-7s to replace locomotives damaged in accidents. Amtrak began phasing out AEM-7s in 2014 as new ACS-64s were delivered. Philadelphia-based SEPTA bought seven AEM-7s (built by Simmering Graz Pauker in Austria) while Maryland Rail Commuter Service (MARC) bought four AEM-7s for Baltimore to Washington services on the Northeast Corridor.

AEM-7 SPECIFICATIONS

Type: High speed passenger electric

Manufacturers: ASEA, Simmering Graz Pauker, Budd and EMD

Years Built: Beginning in 1979

Wheel Arrangement: B-B

Supply Voltage: 11,000 and 12,500 volts at 25 Hz; and 12,500 and 25,000 volts at 60 Hz

Output: 5,695 horsepower

Tractive Effort: 53,300 lbs.

Max. Operating Speed: 125 mph

Weight: 201,600 lbs. (est.)

Overall Length: 51 ft. 2 in.

OPPOSITE: Amtrak's ACS-64 City Sprinter is among the most powerful locomotive operating in the United States.
Brian Solomon

SIEMENS
ACS-64

Amtrak's newest and most powerful locomotives are seventy Siemens-built ACS-64 high-output electrics (numbers 600 to 669) built at Siemens' Sacramento, California, plant. This is an American variation of Siemens' successful Vectron electric. The ACS-64 designation stands for "Amtrak Cities Sprinter 6.4 megawatt output." Amtrak placed the order with Siemens in October 2010, and the first ACS-64 made its debut in May 2013 after rigorous testing.

The ACS-64 is intended to work regional and long-distance trains on the electrified North East Corridor between Boston-New York-Philadelphia-Washington D.C., and Pennsylvania-sponsored Keystone trains between Philadelphia and Harrisburg. The design is intended to haul up to eighteen Amfleet cars at 125 mph. The ACS-64 has allowed the retirement of the HHP-8 and AEM-7 electrics that were the backbone of Amtrak's Regional service for decades. Amtrak's fastest services, marketed as *Acela Express*, will continue to be provided by the fixed-consist, high-speed trains that feature an active tilting mechanism and allow speeds up to 150 mph on select line sections.

The ACS-64 uses European technology, including modern propulsion with the Siemens Sibas 32 control system using high-voltage inverters with IGBT semiconductors, configured for the three NEC AC electrification systems. Traction motors are directly mounted on trucks using rubber fittings to minimize un-sprung weight. The locomotive is equipped with regenerative braking designed to feed 100 percent of braking power back into the overhead catenary. The end cabs are fitted with crash resistant cages designed to comply with FRA-mandated standards for crew safety.

ACS-64 SPECIFICATIONS

Type: High-voltage mainline passenger electric

Manufacturer: Siemens

Years Built: 2012 to present

Wheel Arrangement: B-B

Voltages: 12 kV at 25 Hz, and 12.5 or 25 kV at 60 Hz

Output: 8,580 horsepower

Tractive Effort: 73,600 lbs.

Max. Operating Speed: 125 mph

Weight: 210,000 lbs.

Overall Length: 66 ft. 8 in.

Amtrak ACS-64 number 600 on its first revenue run, February 7, 2014, seen working train 171 from Boston seen passing Milford, Connecticut. Amtrak's ACS-64 "Cities Sprinter" are a variation of the Siemens Vectron series electric and are assembled in California.
Brian Solomon

Bombardier-built ALP-46 4613 pauses at Princeton Junction, New Jersey, with a push-pull set of Bombardier single-level commuter coaches on June 30, 2014. *Brian Solomon*

BOMBARDIER
ALP-46

The ALP-46 was derived from the Adtranz-built German class 101 electric locomotive built exclusively for NJ Transit and related to the modern TRAXX family of electrics and other class 101 derivatives used in Europe, including the extraordinarily powerful IORE locomotives used in iron ore service in Sweden and Norway. The class 101 was introduced in 1996. NJ transit ordered twenty-nine ALP-46 locomotives in 1999 (numbers 4600 to 4628), and during production Bombardier acquired Adtranz in 2001, though al locomotives were built at Kassel, Germany.

This high-horsepower electric uses a standard B-B wheel arrangement, is rated at 7,108 horsepower, weighs 198,400 pounds, and delivers 71,000 pounds starting tractive effort. Using then-state-of-the-art GTO electronics to control three-phase AC traction motors gave the locomotive significantly more starting power than traditional DC traction locomotives; as with other NEC locomotives, they draw power from three different overhead AC systems. The locomotive body is nearly 64 feet long and just over 9 feet 8 inches wide. Top design speed is 100 miles per hour. A more modern variation is the ALP-46A, which has an Isolated Gate Bipolar Transistor (IGBT) traction system and is capable of speeds up to 125 miles per hour. Like the ALP-46, this model is unique to NJ Transit which ordered thirty-six of them in 2008 (numbers 4630 to 4664). Both models are routinely assigned to push-pull consists on NJ Transit suburban trains.

BOMBARDIER ALP-46 SPECIFICATIONS

Type: High-speed passenger electric

Manufacturer: Bombardier

Years Built: Beginning 2002

Railroad: NJ Transit

Wheel Arrangement: B-B

Supply Voltage: 12,500 volts at 25 Hz; and 12,500 and 25,000 volts at 60 Hz

Output: 7,108 horsepower

Tractive Effort: 71,000 lbs. (starting)

Max. Operating Speed: 100 mph

Weight: 198,400 lbs.

Overall Length: 63 ft. 4 in.

BOMBARDIER
ALP-45DP

Bombardier created the dual-mode (or dual power) ALP-45DP by adapting its successful ALP-46A electric locomotive design. The ALP-45DP is a relatively unusual locomotive because it can both work as a diesel-electric and also draw current from overhead AC catenary. While a variety of other dual-mode locomotives have been built for service in the United States, the vast majority of dual-mode types draw external DC power from a line-side third rail. The ALP-45DP locomotive has a sophisticated modern MITRAC® hybrid propulsion system using an Isolated Gate Bipolar Transistor (IGBT) traction converter that enables the locomotive to work from either a pair of onboard diesel engines or overhead wire. The equipment allows the engineer to rapidly switch from one power source to the other while the locomotive is in motion.

Instead of a single large diesel, typical of most North American locomotives, the ALP-45DP has a pair of compact 12-cylinder Caterpillar 3512HP diesels. These energy efficient engines were designed to meet EPA's Tier 3 emission standards. Total output is 4,200 horsepower, however when running HEP to supply power for the passenger cars, only 3,350 horsepower remains for traction. Maximum speed with diesel power is 100 miles per hour. When drawing current from overhead catenary the locomotives are more powerful, with a 5,360 horsepower rating, and are capable of 125 miles per hour.

Total production of the ALP-45DP as of 2015 was fifty-five locomotives. NJ Transit bought thirty-five (numbers 3500 to 3534), with the first built in 2010. Montreal-based Agence Métropolitaine de Transport (AMT) ordered twenty (numbers 1350 to 1369). NJ Transit's locomotives can draw high-voltage AC power from the three different NEC legacy systems: 12,500 volts at 25 Hz; and 12,500 and 25,000 volts at 60 Hz. Montreal's locomotives only use 25,000 volts at 60 Hz.

The locomotives feature a single cab arrangement, standard for most North American diesel electrics but unusual for straight electrics, which typically have cabs at each end. They are just over 71 feet 6 inches long and slightly more than 14 feet 5 inches tall. Axle weight based on NJ Transit's order is 71,000 pounds. NJ Transit's

BOMBARDIER ALP-45DP SPECIFICATIONS

Type: dual mode overhead electric/diesel passenger locomotive

Manufacturer: Bombardier

Years Built: Beginning 2011

Wheel Arrangement: B-B

Input Voltage: 12,500 volts at 25 Hz; and 12,500 and 25,000 volts at 60 Hz.

Output: 5,360 horsepower (electric)

Tractive Effort: NA

Max. Operating Speed: 125 mph (electric), 100 mph (diesel)

Weight: 284,000 lbs.

Overall Length: 71 ft. 6 in.

ABOVE: NJ Transit ALP-45DP 4506 makes a station stop on the Raritan Valley Line at Cranford, New Jersey, in June 2015. *Brian Solomon*

LEFT: Montreal-based Agence Métropolitaine de Transport (AMT) has twenty ALP-45DP dual-mode locomotives for suburban passenger services through the Mount Royal Tunnel electrified at 25kV 60Hz. *Dan Howard*

ALP-45DPs were ordered to be fully compatible with its existing passenger car fleet and have been routinely assigned to work Northeast Corridor, Boonton, and Raritan Valley routes, among other lines.

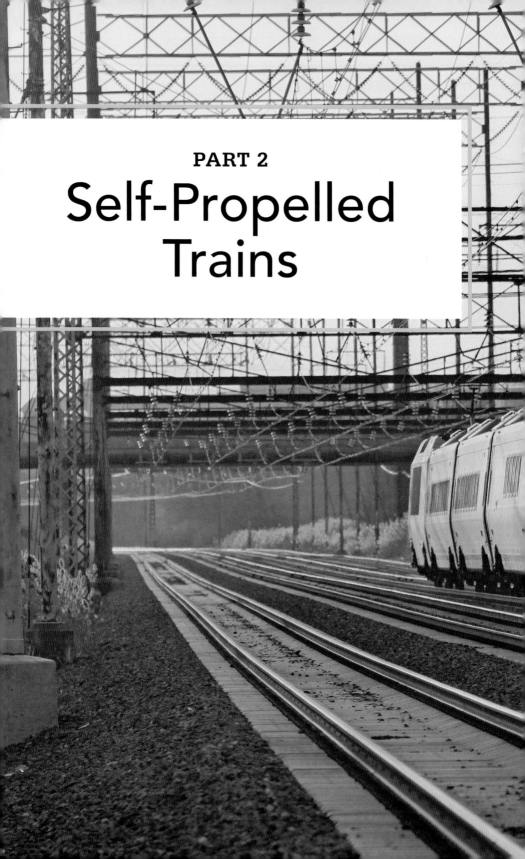

PART 2
Self-Propelled Trains

INTRODUCTION

Traditionally, trains were locomotive hauled. In modern North American practice, where extremely powerful diesel-electric locomotives are the rule, most trains still involve locomotives and self-propelled passenger trains are only used in limited circumstances. The opposite is true in most of Europe and in many densely populated Asian nations, where high-density passenger operations represent the dominant railway activity. In those situations self-propelled trains are by far the most common variety of equipment. It seems reasonable, then, that when modern self-propelled trains are used in North America, they tend to be adaptations of European and Asian equipment built by multinational railcar manufacturers.

One of the advantages of electrification is the ability to operate electric multiple units, where each passenger car is individually powered by traction motors on the car. In practice, it is common to pair or group cars in a set coupled semi-permanently, both to minimize the number of control cabs (which are costly and occupy space that could be better used for passenger seating) and to reduce the overall weight of the vehicle. Distributing motors throughout a train allows for smoother operation and rapid acceleration. An advantage of the multiple units system is that train size can be easily adjusted to suit the specific demands of service. Short trains can be operated off-peak, while longer trains can be coupled together for

On the right is a classic Budd Rail Diesel Car that was built in large numbers between 1949 and 1962. On the left is rare example of the Colorado Rail Car, a modern diesel multiple-unit design to meet FRA crash-worthiness standards. *Jack May*

PREVIOUS PAGE: A Washington D.C.-bound *Acela Express* blitzes Marcus Hook, Pennsylvania, at 125 mph on January 17, 2015. *Brian Solomon*

Diesel multiple units are rare in the United States, but NJ Transit's River Line service is an exception. This uses a fleet of Swiss-designed Stadler GTW 2/6. *Jack May*

rush hour schedules. If one car develops a flaw, if can be easily removed from the train without complicated shop procedures.

Today, New York and Philadelphia area suburban operations are mostly operated using electric multiple units, while Montreal and Chicago feature some electric multiple unit operations. Denver is in the process of building an electric suburban line, which will use Hyundai Rotem cars similar to those bought by Philadelphia-based SEPTA.

High-speed long-distance self-propelled trains have been rare in the United States. Spurred forward by the enormous success of the original Japanese Shinkansen in 1964, Pennsylvania Railroad and Budd used federal funds to develop the high-speed Metroliner, a 120-miles-per-hour

emu designed for express long-distance service between New York and Washington. Amtrak inherited the cars and operation. The original Metroliner cars were replaced by locomotive-hauled trains in the early 1980s, while Metroliner cab cars were rebuilt for push-pull service on locomotive-powered trains. The self-propelled high-speed long-distance electric train was revived in the late 1990s with development of the *Acela Express* trains, based on French and Canadian technologies. These remain as the fastest trains in North America and are Amtrak's only self-propelled trains. They use semi-permanently coupled high-output power cars at both ends of custom-designed six car trains.

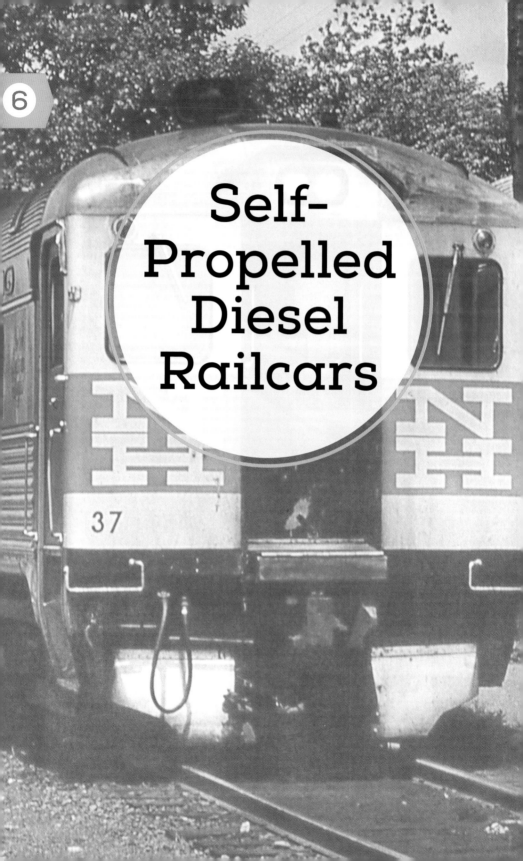

Self-Propelled Diesel Railcars

BUDD
RAIL DIESEL CAR

The Philadelphia-based Budd Company served as a
significant supplier of passenger cars beginning in the
1930s. In 1949, it introduced its Rail Diesel Car (commonly
known as an RDC), which like its other passenger cars was
constructed using Budd's patented shot-welded stainless-
steel design, featuring characteristic side fluting.

Unlike the old gas-electric cars from the 1910s and
1920s, which were largely single-ended machines designed
to operate singly (or perhaps haul a trailer or two), Budd's
RDCs were double-ended and designed for multiple-unit
operation. Some RDCs were intended for branch line and/
or suburban work, while others were used for long-distance
runs. Budd offered several car configurations: the RDC-1
used its compartment entirely for passenger seating; the
RDC-2 included a baggage compartment; the RDC-3 had
baggage and Railway Post Office sections in addition to
coach seats; the RDC-4 was strictly a baggage car/RPO
unit; the RDC-9 was a cab-less variety intended to work as a
center car between two other units. New Haven ordered a
specialized RDC train for its *Roger Williams* service.

The RDC was offered as a means of reducing operating
costs and was especially useful for lightly traveled routes
and suburban lines. Budd built a total of 398 by the early

BUDD RDC-1
SPECIFICATIONS

Type: Self-propelled diesel-
hydraulic passenger railcar

Manufacturer: Budd
Company

Years Built: 1949-1960s

Wheel Arrangement:
1A-A1

Engine: Two GM 6-110
diesels

Output: 275-300
horsepower

Tractive Effort: NA

Max. Operating Speed:
85 mph

Weight: 108,000 lbs.

Overall Length: 85 ft.

New Haven Railroad was a large buyer of Budd's RDC. This car was still relatively new when
photographed in July 1960. *Richard Jay Solomon*

ABOVE: Metro-North SPV-2000s rest at Poughkeepsie, New York, on June 15, 1986. *Brian Solomon*

LEFT: Bellefonte Historical Railroad 9153 is a classic example of a late-build Budd RDC1. *Dan Howard*

1960s, and some of the largest fleets were bought by New Haven and Boston & Maine. In 1971, Amtrak inherited twenty-four RDCs, which were largely assigned to New England services, where one pair operated until 1986. Boston-based MBTA, which inherited many cars from Penn-Central and Boston & Maine and added to its collection RDCs from Canadian Pacific and Reading Company, ended up assigning RDCs to push-pull sets with a diesel-electric at one end. Later, it had some RDCs rebuilt into un-powered passenger coaches.

Although the RDC is no longer a common type of equipment, as of 2015 a few operational cars survive in remote services on VIA Rail in Canada and the Alaska Railroad. A few work on tourist railroads.

In 1978, Budd reintroduced the self-propelled passenger car with its SPV-2000, which used the Metro-shell body common to its Metroliner EMU and Amfleet cars. It was powered by a 360-horsepower General Motors Detroit Diesel engine. Connecticut Department of Transportation purchased thirteen SPV-2000s that were briefly operated by Amtrak on the New Haven-Hartford-Springfield shuttle, and by Metro-North suburban branch line runs to Waterbury and Danbury. Metro-North also operated SPV-2000s on its former New York Central lines.

SIEMENS DESIRO VT 642

The Siemens Desiro family covers a range of regional and commuter passenger trains. The Desiro VT 642 is a two-unit lightweight diesel-mechanical multiple unit. Between 2000 and 2003, Siemens delivered 233 of these to Deutsche Bahn (German Railways) for local passenger service. In 2006-2007, a dozen nearly identical cars were built for the new *Sprinter* service operated by the San Diego-area North County Transit District (NITD). This an unusual example of a European-style passenger service began in March 2008, largely serving the 22-mile former Santa Fe branch line between Oceanside and Escondido, California. *Sprinter* began operations using regular-interval service: trains depart terminals every half hour weekdays, and every hour on weekends, with trains stopping at fifteen conveniently located stations along the line. The *Sprinter*'s VG642s are powered by a pair of 420 horsepower turbo-charged intercooled 6-cylinder diesel engines and transmit power using five-speed torque converters. A single engineer may operate several VG642 Desiros coupled together, which allows for longer trains during peak travel periods. The Desiro's low floor entrance design allow passengers to board trains quickly without assistance from on-board train staff, and handicapped passengers can access trains without specialized equipment, high-level platforms or prolonged station stops.

Unlike their cousins in Germany, which have a top speed of 75 miles per hour, NITD's VT642s *Sprinters* have a design speed of just 55 miles per hour, which is ample for local conditions. Other nominal differences include a more powerful air-conditioning system and the omission of first-class seating. NITD's VT642s are similar to other Siemens Desiro diesel railcars, including Desiro Classic models used in Denmark, Hungary, and Romania. Unlike on European railways where lightweight cars such as the VT642 can operate freely on lines served by other types of rail traffic, American railroads have different philosophies and requirements for signaling and rail safety that impose more restrictive procedures when lightweight railcars share track space with freight trains. *Sprinter* and freight trains must use a system of temporal (time) separation to ensure

DESIRO VT642 SPECIFICATIONS

Type: Diesel-mechanical multiple unit

Manufacturer: Siemens

Years Built: Beginning 2000

Wheel Arrangement: NA

Engine: Two turbo-charged 6-cylinder diesels

Output: 420 horsepower

Tractive Effort: NA

Seats: 128

Max. Operating Speed: 55 mph

Weight: NA

Overall Length: NA

that no VT642s use the lines at the same time freight trains are operating. Typically, freights serve local customers along the line at night.

San Diego area's North County Transit District markets its Oceanside-Escondido service as Sprinter, and operates it with a fleet Desiro VT642 diesel multiple units built by Siemens AG Transportation Systems. *Jack May*

STADLER GTW RAILCAR

Stadler Rail Ag is a Swiss-based railcar manufacturer. Among its many products is the GTW (*Galenk Triebwagen*) line of articulated modular railcars. This style can be ordered either as a diesel-electric powered car or with electric propulsion only. Key to the design is the centrally located power segment (or module). Diesel cars have a compact MTU 500kW (670 horsepower) engine that transmits power via a three-phase electrical generator and IGBT power converter to a pair of asynchronous traction motors. The only powered axles are the pair below the central power segment; the outside axles at the ends of the car are unpowered.

Since 2004, three American operators have bought small fleets of Stadler GTW diesel-electric cars. The first, NJ Transit, bought twenty GTW 2/6 DMUs featuring a boxy body style for service on its River Line between Trenton and Camden, New Jersey. The Denton County Transportation Authority and Capitol Metro in Austin use the cars on modern transit lines in Texas. These cars also carry the GTW 2/6 DMU designation, but use a body style similar to Stadler's Flirt line of equipment (the larger heavier railcar design that is common on European railways).

GTW 2/6 DMU SPECIFICATIONS (NJ TRANSIT SPECS)

Type: Diesel-electric multiple unit railcar

Years Built: 2002-2003 (for NJT)

Manufacturer: Stadler

Wheel Arrangement: 2-B-2

Engine: MTU diesel

Output: 670 horsepower

Tractive Effort: 15,737 lbs.

Max. Operating Speed: 68 mph

Seats: 70

Weight: 129,630 lbs.

ABOVE: The Austin, Texas, Capitol Metro operates a 32-mile suburban service using six Stadler GTW 2/6 diesel rail cars acquired in 2008. *Jack May*

LEFT: The Denton County Transportation Authority bought eleven Stadler GTW 2/6 diesel multiple units in May 2009. *Jack May*

PREVIOUS: NJ Transit's 20 Stadler GTW 2/6 diesel multiple units at Delanco, New Jersey use a different body style than typical European versions of the same equipment. *Jack May*

Electric Multiple Units

SILVERLINERS IV/JERSEY
ARROWS

Since the mid-1970s, one of the most common varieties of suburban equipment operating in New Jersey and eastern Pennsylvania include the electric multiple units built by General Electric using stainless steel body shells by Avco. Units operated by the South Eastern Pennsylvania Transportation Authority are GE model MA-1H known on SEPTA as Silverliner IVs, which follow a family of similar cars built in the 1960s known as Silverliner IIs (built by the St. Louis Car Company) and Silverliner IIIs (built by the Budd Company). SEPTA's cars were built between 1974 and 1976 for Philadelphia-area electric suburban operation on Penn-Central's former Pennsylvania Railroad and Reading Company lines and remain a core portion of SEPTA's heavy rail fleet. There are two varieties: double-ended single cars, and married pairs of single-ended cars.

The Jersey Arrow III units are very similar, built by GE between 1977-1978 as model MA-1G, for the New Jersey Department of Transportation and today operated by NJ Transit on former Lackawanna and Pennsylvania Railroad electrified lines. NJ Transit single cars with cabs at both ends are numbered in the 1304 to 1333 series, and married pairs with cab-less ends coupled together numbered 1334 to 1533. One of the principal external differences with the NJT Arrow IIIs is the central door, which distinguishes these from SEPTA's cars with no center door. NJ Transit's fleet of older Jersey Arrow II units was largely scrapped prior to 2001.

SEPTA SILVERLINER IV SPECIFICATIONS

Type: Electric multiple unit

Manufacturer: General Electric and Avco

Years Built: 1974-1976

Wheel Arrangement: NA

Supply Voltage: 12,000 volts at 25Hz, 12,500 and 25,000 volts at 60Hz.

Output: NA

Tractive Effort: NA

Seats: 126

Max. Operating Speed: 85 mph

Weight: 120,600 lbs.

Overall Length: 85 ft.

OPPOSITE: SEPTA Silverliner IVs. *Brian Solomon*

BELOW: NJ Transit 1306, an example of a single Arrow-III electric multiple unit, discharges passengers at Princeton Junction, New Jersey. *Brian Solomon*

NIPPON SHARYO
MODEL MC SINGLE LEVEL EMUS

In the early twentieth century, Chicago, South Shore & South Bend—known as the South Shore—was one of three large interurban electric systems serving Chicago under the management of Samuel Insull. Today it is America's last surviving overhead-electric interurban-line (energized at 1,500 volt DC). The Northern Indiana Commuter Transportation District (NICTD) was formed in 1973 to subsidize South Shore passenger services; it assumed passenger operations in 1990, although the service is still identified with the traditional South Shore name. Electric trains use a 90-mile route from South Bend via Michigan City, Indiana, to Chicago, reaching Metra's Millennium station via trackage rights on the Metra Electric District (formerly Illinois Central. See next.) from a junction at Kensington.

Between 1981 and 1983, NICTD replaced South Shore's 1920s-era steel-interurban cars with forty-four model Mc electric multiple-units built by Nippon Sharyo. The modern stainless-steel cars represented a stark contrast to the traditional cars that had plied the line for more than five decades. NICTD bought another seventeen cars in 1993. In 2000, Nippon Sharyo supplied ten more similar-looking, but more modern type McW Model 100 cars. These are two feet shorter and use a modern inverter type electrical propulsion system.

MODEL MC ELECTRIC MULTIPLE UNITS SPECIFICATIONS

Type: Single level electric multiple unit

Manufacturer: Nippon Sharyo

Years Built: 1981-1983

Supply Voltage: 1,500 volt DC

Output: NA

Tractive Effort: NA

Max. Operating Speed: 79 mph

Seats: 90/93

Weight: 118,000 lbs.

Overall Length: 85 ft.

Nippon Sharyo Model Mc emus work the South Shore at Michigan City, Indiana.
Brian Solomon

NIPPON SHARYO
BI-LEVEL EMUS

Metra Electric operates former Illinois Central suburban services, wired with 1,500 volt DC overhead, running from Millennium station (formerly IC's Randolph Street) to University Park, with branches to Blue Island and South Chicago. In 2005, Nippon Sharyo converted twenty-six Metra stainless steel bi-level gallery-style commuter cars to type-MC model 1200 self-propelled operation with the addition of electric inverter-controlled propulsions equipment. These cars were the first modern Highliner class electric-multiple units and are arranged in married pairs. In service they may run in trains up to eight cars. The basic seating arrangement and overall car configuration was unchanged. Typically there are 128 seats per car, with slightly fewer on cars arranged for wheelchair access. Control cabs are on the upper level. Metra added another 106 similar cars between 2012 and 2013.

In 2009 The Northern Indiana Commuter Transportation District bought fourteen similar cars for service on the South Shore. These feature a slightly different body style and a revised door arrangement to facilitate the specific loading characteristics of the South Shore route. The cars are adorned with traditional South Shore maroon and traction orange logos.

MC MODEL 1200 ELECTRIC MULTIPLE UNITS SPECIFICATIONS

Type: Electric multiple unit

Manufacturer: Nippon Sharyo

Years Built: 2005-2013

Total number of cars: 132

Supply Voltage: 1,500 volts DC

Output: NA

Tractive Effort: NA

Max. Operating Speed: 79 mph

Seats: 120/128

Weight: 143,800 lbs.

Overall Length: 85 ft.

The newest equipment from Northern Indiana Commuter Transportation District, which operates service on the South Shore route, is a small modern fleet of Nippon Sharyo stainless-steel bi-levels. *Tom Kline*

ACELA EXPRESS

Unique to Amtrak's Northeast Corridor (NEC) are the custom built High-Speed Electric Trainsets designed for *Acela Express* services between Washington and Boston. Twenty complete train-sets were built by a consortium of Alstom and Bombardier between 1998 and 2000. They were introduced into traffic following opening of the fully electrified trackage between New Haven, Connecticut, and Boston in January 2000, with the first Acela service runs inaugurated on December 10, 2000.

The trains are powered with Alstom's three-phase propulsion system originally engineered for France's advanced Trains à Grande Vitesse (TGV). The trains are bidirectional with locomotive power cars (model type PC, numbers 2000 to 2039), and these are arranged at each end of a set of six passenger cars coupled semi-permanently, although the design allows for trains up to ten cars. Owing to the complicated history of NEC electrification, these power cars are designed to work with the line's different AC high-voltage schemes: 12kV at 25Hz; and 12.5kV or 25kV at 60Hz. Each power car has four asynchronous AC motors, one motor per axle, and is rated to deliver 6,169 continuous horsepower for total of 12,338 horsepower.

Top design speed is 165 miles per hour, but as of 2015 the trains are limited to 150 miles per hour in revenue service. Top running speeds are only presently allowed on

ACELA EXPRESS SPECIFICATIONS

Type: High-Speed Electric Trainset

Manufacturer: Alstom with Bombardier

Years Built: 1998-2000

Wheel Arrangement: Power car B-B, passenger cars 2-2

Supply Voltage: 12,000 volts at 25Hz; and 12,500 volts or 25,000 volts at 60Hz

Output: 12,338 horsepower (provided by two power cars)

Tractive Effort: Starting 49,400 lbs.

Seats: 240 business class, 44 first class, plus café car

Max. Operating Speed: 165 mph, 150 mph in traffic

Weight: Power car 200,000 lbs. each, end coach 129,000 lbs., coach/first class coach 127,000 lbs., café 132,000 lbs.

Overall Length: Power car, 69 ft. 7 3/8 in.; typical train with power cars and 6 coaches, 660 ft. 4.75 in.

Amtrak's *Acela*-service high-speed train-sets use power cars at each end. *Brian Solomon*

Amtrak's Acela Express High Speed Train Sets are the fastest trains in North America and are allowed to travel up to 150 mph in revenue service. *Brian Solomon*

select line segments between New Haven and Boston, but track upgrading between Newark and Trenton, New Jersey, may soon allow the trains to reach their top potential speed. In order provide greater passenger comfort at high speed through curves, *Acela Express* HST trains use an active tilting mechanism originally developed for Canada's Light Rapid Comfortable (LRC). Notably, only the passenger cars tilt.

Passenger cars were built in four variations: end-coach (numbers 3400 to 3419), coach (3500 to 3559), café (3300 to 3319), and first class (3200 to 3219), with three coaches on each six-car train and one each of the other types. The trains are marketed as an upscale service with accelerated schedules and carry only business class and first class passengers. Amtrak's *Acela Express* trains provide its up-market Northeast Corridor service aimed to compete with regional airlines in the Boston-New York-Washington market. In addition, on the same route, Amtrak operates locomotive-hauled regional trains with Amfleet that are nominally slower and priced more affordably.

BOMBARDIER
M7 ELECTRIC MULTIPLE UNITS

One of the largest and most intensively used types passenger equipment in the United States is the M7 class electric multiple unit. Bombardier built two separate fleets for New York Metropolitan Transportation Authority to work Long Island Rail Road and Metro North lines from New York City, totaling 1,172 M7 electric multiple units built in married pairs, acquired to replace the worn out fleets of 1970s-era Metropolitan series cars. Although they largely share the same specifications, there are notable differences between LIRR and MN fleets; they are maintained and operated separately as result of the heritage of their respective operators.

Long Island Rail Road is America's largest suburban railroad. It uses an over-running third rail on its electrified lines, stemming from LIRR's historic affiliation with Pennsylvania Railroad, serving Pennsylvania Station in Manhattan (which originally used third rail for PRR locomotive-hauled trains through its Hudson tunnels). Metro-North's electrified operations are centered at Grand Central Terminal, using a distinctive style of under-running third rail developed by New York Central and General Electric in the early years of the twentieth century. MN assigns its M7s to service on its former New York Central third-rail routes: the Harlem Line to Southeast Station (north of Brewster, New York); and Hudson Line to Croton-Harmon.

M7 EMU SPECIFICATIONS

Type: Electric multiple units

Manufacturer: Bombardier

Years Built: Beginning 2002 for LIRR, beginning 2004 for MN

Wheel Arrangement: NA

Supply Voltage: 750 volts DC

Output: NA

Tractive Effort: NA

Seats: 110 in A car; 101 in B car

Max. Operating Speed: 100 mph

Weight: NA

Overall Length: 85 ft.

Width: 10 ft. 6 in.

Metro-North assigns its Bombardier-built M7 electric multiple-units to suburban service on former New York Central System Hudson and Harlem Lines. *Walter E. Zullig*

KAWASAKI RAIL CAR
M8 ELECTRIC MULTIPLE UNITS

In 2006, the State of Connecticut and the New York Metropolitan Transportation Authority's Metro North Railroad jointly ordered the first M8 electric multiple unit cars from Kawasaki Rail Car. These were specifically designed for service on former New Haven Railroad electrified routes between New York City's Grand Central Terminal and New Haven, Connecticut, plus service on the New Canaan Branch. They are also intended eventually to serve Shore Line East services east of New Haven to New London.

Owing to the four different electrification standards on these routes, the M8s can draw power from three forms of high voltage AC with overhead catenary and under-running third rail energized at 750 volts DC for access to Grand Central. The cars were acquired to permit gradual retirement of 1970s and 1980s-era Metropolitan series electric multiple units. By July 2015, Kawasaki had delivered 405 units—380 married-pairs and 25 single double-ended cars—so the last of the older cars are finally being withdrawn.

Kawasaki built the first twenty-five units at its factory in Kobe, Japan, while the remaining units were constructed domestically at its facility in Lincoln, Nebraska. The M8s introduced an improved passenger compartment with brighter lighting, larger windows, and more comfortable seats. As with the older Cosmopolitan/Metropolitan series of cars, the M8 features two by three seating.

M8 EMU SPECIFICATIONS

Equipment Type: Electric multiple unit

Manufacturer: Kawasaki Rail Car

Years Built: 2010-2015

Wheel Arrangement: NA

Supply Voltage: 750 volts DC (3rd rail), 12,000 volts 25 Hz, 25,000 volts 60 Hz

Output: NA

Tractive Effort: NA

Seats: 111 A car; 101 B car

Max. Operating Speed: 100 mph

Weight: NA

Overall Length: 85 ft.

A set of fresh Kawasaki M8s on the New Haven Line glide through the snow at Milford, Connecticut. *Brian Solomon*

HYUNDAI-ROTEM
SILVERLINER V

Philadelphia-based Southeastern Pennsylvania Transportation Authority introduced its new Silverliner V electric multiple unit trains in 2010. Designed by Korean railcar manufacturer Hyundai-Rotem and constructed in Philadelphia using locally manufactured parts, the cars are intended to work all of SEPTA's Regional Rail lines (as distinguished from its urban rapid transit and trolley lines). The order for 120 cars was completed in 2013.

Silverliner V is a bold new design with smooth, stainless-steel bodies and large windows. The cars benefit from state-of-the-art features including side-of-car lit-destination signs, two pairs of exit doors per car, and room for bicycles on board. The cars feature modern regenerative braking that turn the AC traction motors into generators to supply current to help power lighting and climate control and feed current back into the overhead catenary. The stylish interior design was tailored to SEPTA's requirements. On-board digital display screens provide up-to-date rider information as the trains roll along.

The Silverliner V cars allowed SEPTA to replace its 1960s-era Silverliner II and III electric multiple units (see above). It operates three variations, including double-ended cars that can work singly or in multiple with other Silverliner Vs. Denver's Regional Transport District has ordered sixty-six similar cars for a new electrified service to begin in 2016.

SILVERLINER V SPECIFICATIONS

Type: Electric multiple unit

Manufacturer: Hyundai-Rotem

Years Built: Beginning in 2010

Wheel Arrangement: NA

Supply Voltage: 11,500 volts 25 Hz; 12,500 and 25,000 volts at 60Hz

Output: NA

Tractive Effort: NA

Seats: 107 (single car)

Max. Operating Speed: 100 mph

Weight: 124,280 lbs. (single car)

Overall Length: 85 ft.

A set of new ROTEM-built Silverliner Vs approach Ardmore, Pennsylvania.
Brian Solomon

PART 3
Passenger and Freight Cars

INTRODUCTION

Historically, American passenger services were provided by the privately operated railroad companies that each ordered its own equipment based upon its specific requirements. This led to a great variety of different equipment, but established standards made most passenger cars compatible with one another except in unusual circumstances.

A handful of manufacturers built equipment for most railroads in the United States. During the mid-twentieth century, Pullman-Standard was the largest car supplier, and was famous for its nineteenth century development of the sleeping car. Other traditional builders included American Car & Foundry and St. Louis Car Company. The Philadelphia Budd Company, a one-time automotive

manufacturing supplier, entered railcar business with its invention of streamlined lightweight trains in the 1930s that led it to become one of the principle innovators to North American car design. It cars were manufactured using a patented welded stainless steel process, and some were so well built that they remain in regular service after more than six decades. Today, welded stainless steel construction is a standard feature of most passenger car designs.

During the latter twentieth century, American passenger railroading underwent multifaceted changes. Widespread automobile ownership and changes to travel patterns had made virtually all passenger services unprofitable. As ridership declined, railroads discontinued

A mixed consist of Viewliner sleeping cars, a heritage Budd-built diner, and Amfleet coaches roll east on Amtrak's Lake Shore Limited near Buffalo, New York. *Brian Solomon*

PREVIOUS PAGE: Low-profile VIA Rail LRC tilting cars pass Bombardier bi-levels in Toronto. *Brian Solomon*

Amtrak TALGO trains wait between runs at Portland Union Station in Portland, Oregon. In the lead are Amtrak's NPCU "Cabbage" units, which had converted into unpowered cab-control cars from old F40PH diesels. *Scott Lothes*

trains and many routes lost scheduled passenger services. Between the 1960s and the 1980s, operation of passenger service made the transition from private railroad operation to that by public agencies.

In 1971, Amtrak assumed operation of most remaining long-distance passenger trains, a move that coincided with a drastic reduction of the number of trains operated nationally. A similar move occurred in Canada in the late-1970s, when VIA Rail assumed operation of Canadian National and Canadian Pacific long-distance services. Commuter rail underwent a parallel transformation, as cities and regional authorities first began subsidizing train operations, and then ultimately took charge of operations and transportation planning.

In the mid-1980s, passenger rail began to enjoy a revival. As urban highways became increasingly congested, rail commutation gained popularity. Not only was the level of service improved, but the route structure was expanded and new commuter networks formed. Cities that had never enjoyed commuter rail, or had lost all passenger service decades earlier, began investing in modern suburban railways.

Nationally, Amtrak's intercity route structure often underwent nominal changes as result of period budget shortfalls. Yet, provisions in Amtrak's charter facilitated expansion where individual states shared costs. Several states, notably California, Oregon, and Washington, invested heavily in long-distance trains.

GATX is the reporting mark for General American Transportation. Exceptionally large cars such as this GATX prototype four-truck 96,500-gallon tank car are unusual in North American practice. This car is displayed at the National Museum of Transportation in St. Louis. *Brian Solomon*

During this period of decline and revival, the traditional passenger car manufacturers exited the business. In their place, international companies entered the North American market. Today most new passenger cars are supplied by Asian and European railcar builders, although to fulfill "Buy-American" requirements, cars are assembled locally. As a result, North American cars benefit from a variety of designs and technological innovations introduced overseas. Passenger car manufacturers often also built transit equipment, which while covered separately in this book, tends to involve the same essential technology as heavy-rail passenger cars, and it's not unusual to find rapid transit and heavy railcars being constructed side by side in the same factories.

North American passenger cars are typically about 85 feet long and tend to be significantly larger (and heavier) than comparable equipment in continental Europe, due to the generous North America loading gauge, higher minimum axle weights, and strict crash-worthiness standards. Double-deck designs, which took a toehold in the 1950s, are now dominant in many areas. Single-level equipment is still required on many lines in the East owing to historical clearance restrictions, especially on portions of the heavily traveled North East Corridor.

Tilting trains allow greater speed on existing infrastructure, and so Canada's LRC system and the Spanish TALGO style of tilting train have found limited markets. Amtrak's Acela Express high-speed train (detailed in Chapter 2) uses the LRC tilting technology.

Long-distance equipment differs from that used in suburban service in a variety of ways. Commuter trains make the most of interior space to get the greatest number of passengers on board, and have minimal frills. Since long-distance services are often marketed on the train-riding experience rather than basic transportation, they focus on passenger comfort, have more space for luggage, and tend to include dining facilities, ranging from full sit-down dining cars with table service to buffet and café cars. The heyday of the sleeping car has long since passed, yet Amtrak still operates more than a dozen overnight trains between principal cities. Western long-distance trains (plus services in the East that benefit from greater clearances, such as the Auto train and Capitol Limited) use bi-level Superliner cars. Most eastern trains use Amfleet and Viewliner equipment. Recent purchases of the latter finally are replacing the last of inherited Budd-built Heritage diners and baggage cars.

The North American freight car fleet is a vast sea of rolling steel. By one estimate, the entire railcar fleet on rails in Canada, Mexico, and the United States consists of 1.6 million vehicles, with as many as 1.25 million cars on the move at any one time. Based on this number, if you were to witness 200 freight cars passing each day (and never spotted the same car twice) it would take you 22 years to observe the whole fleet! While there are a huge number of cars, and a great variety of different car designs, most cars are represented by just a few basic types, with each type consisting of sub-types necessary for individual service requirements.

Classic types of cars include: the basic boxcar, refrigerated boxcars, hoppers, gondolas, flats, and tank cars. While each is explored in greater detail in the following pages, it is impossible for a book of this size to list all active variations for each car, let alone address the myriad historical variations or present a complete visual catalog of the North American freight car pool.

Over the years the freight car fleet has undergone a continual transformation as sizes and types have evolved to meet changes in shipping requirements, as well as fundamental changes in the way North American railroads have moved freight.

Historically, railroads were common-carriers and moved almost every conceivable type of freight, small and large. Competition from other modes, especially over-the-road trucking, has resulted in railroads focusing on just a few primary types of traffic: largely heavy bulk commodities such as coal, grain, mineral ores, petroleum, timber products, automotive components and finished automobiles and trucks; and the long-distance transport of intermodal trailers and containers.

Since the 1950s, railroads have moved away from this traditional model as trucks claimed the most lucrative high-value traffic and small shipments. Beginning in the 1950s, railroads tried to reclaim high-value business and tap off-line customers by developing intermodal traffic, and this process accelerated as a result of deregulation (culminating with the passage of the Staggers Act in 1980). Initially, intermodal shipments were handled one carload at time, with traditional freights hauling loads with a truck trailer or two chained to a flatcar. As this business grew, specialized intermodal cars were developed and railroads began operating dedicated intermodal trains between specialized terminals. Another change was that bulk traffic was focused in unit-train shipments running directly from origin to destination.

The freight car fleet evolved in several distinct ways as railroad customers evolved into intermodal shippers and huge bulk customers moving unit trains. Once the backbone of railroad shipping, the traditional boxcar has diminished, while specialized car types have come to dominate North American rail freight operations. The freight fleet has contracted despite a swell in freight shipments (in 2009, railroads moved 1.7 billion tons of freight, a far greater volume than during the peak years of World War II).

Commuter Rail

GALLERY CARS

Bi-level gallery-style suburban passenger cars have been
built for commuter services in Chicago, the San Francisco
Bay area, and several other metropolitan areas. Chicago,
Burlington & Quincy ordered the first gallery cars from
Budd for its Chicago-Aurora service in 1949. These cars
established a pattern emulated by several builders over
the last seven decades, characterized by a high-capacity
arrangement facilitated by central low-level double doors
to allow rapid loading and unloading, with an open bi-level
seating arrangement that features 2 x 2 seating on the
lower level and rows of single seats on the gallery level.
The gallery rows are cantilever-supported from the walls
and ceiling to minimize obstructions on the lower level.
Budd's original cars were delivered in 1950, and by 1965
Burlington's entire fleet was comprised of gallery cars.
Typical of Budd passenger car design, CB&Q's cars were
constructed from shot-welded stainless steel. Similar cars
were built for Milwaukee Road and Rock Island services.

Chicago & North Western, operator of one of Chicago's
most significant important suburban commuter services,
first bought high-capacity smooth-side steel gallery cars
built by St. Louis Car Company in 1955. Interestingly,
these cars briefly overlapped with steam operations.
C&NW's later gallery cars were built by Pullman-Standard
and were among the earliest modern cars equipped for
push-pull service and modern head-end heating and
lighting technology. It also operated deluxe bi-level
gallery-cars on its long-distance trains between Chicago,
Green Bay, and points north. In 1955, Southern Pacific
bought a similar fleet of Pullman-Standard gallery cars
for San Francisco-San Jose commute services. These
measured 15 feet 8 inches tall and 85 feet long with a total
passenger capacity of 145 passengers.

In the early 1970s, push-pull operations supplanted
most traditional locomotive-hauled suburban services
in the Chicago-area, and cab-control cars and additional
stainless steel bi-level coaches were bought for
Chicago area service, as these services were undergoing
a transition from private to public operation. In 1984,
Chicago's suburban operations were rebranded as Metra.
Meanwhile, a similar transition was underway in California,
as operation of SP's Commute operations was gradually
assumed by public organizations and marketed as Cal
Train. As part of this change, a fleet of seventy-three new
stainless steel gallery cars was built by Japanese supplier

SOUTHERN PACIFIC GALLERY CARS SPECIFICATIONS

Type: Bi-level commuter coach

Manufacturer: Pullman-Standard

Years Built: Beginning 1955

Seats: 145

Overall Length: 85 ft.

Height: 15 ft. 8 in.

Beginning in 1950, Chicago,
Burlington & Quincy was
the first to use gallery-style
commuter rail cars. *Brian Solomon*

Washington, DC-based Virginia Rail Express has bought two orders of Nippon Sharyo stainless-steel gallery-style bi-level passenger cars. A VRE set working cab-car first approaches Alexandria on a January 2015 evening. *Walter E. Zullig*

Nippon-Sharyo between 1984 and 1987, and an additional twenty cars were built in 1998. To meet modern standards established by the Americans with Disabilities Act, these later Nippon Sharyo cars came equipped with fewer seats to make room for disabled accommodations and bicycles. Chicago's Metra ordered large fleets of Nippon-Sharyo stainless steel gallery cars beginning in 1994. While similar in general external appearance to the original CB&Q cars, the most modern Metra gallery cars feature disabled-friendly designs. In addition, an electric multiple-unit variation was acquired for Metra Electric and later for South Shore services. Washington DC-based Virginia Rail Express bought seventy-one Nippon-Sharyo gallery cars built between 2006 and 2009.

Many of Metra's older gallery cars, including all of the smooth-side cars, have been retired, although some were sold to other operations, such as Wisconsin & Southern, which used them in excursion service and on Madison-based football specials.

HAWKER-SIDDELEY/ BOMBARDIER
BI-LEVEL COMMUTER CARS

Today, one of the most common types of North American commuter rail equipment is the tapered-end bi-level commuter car built by Bombardier (and its predecessors), used by a dozen different suburban rail-service operators. Toronto-centered GO Transit has been one of the most innovative suburban passenger carriers since its unprecedented late-era start up in 1967. (Originally GO Transit was the marketing name for Government of Ontario Transit, today GO Transit is a division of Metrolinx, an agency that coordinates public transport in the area of Toronto-Hamilton, Ontario.) GO was an early user of push-pull train sets and from its beginning embraced head-end power (HEP) supply. Less than a decade after it began, GO Transit's rail ridership was on the rise and it sought greater passenger train capacity. In 1976, it placed an order with Canadian manufacturer Hawker-Siddeley for eighty bi-level passenger cars. These featured a steel frame, but a riveted aluminum body with distinctive tapered ends set them apart from everything else on the move in North America. The first cars were delivered in 1977. Since that time, this essential design has gone through eight different production series (design variations) and have been produced by three builders.

Hawker-Siddeley produced the first two series, with the second series beginning production in 1983. Significantly, this series involved the introduction of a cab-control

BI-LEVEL SERIES 1 SPECIFICATIONS

Type: Bi-level commuter coach

Manufacturer: Hawker-Siddeley

Years Built: 1976–1978

Seats: 162

Weight: 109,130 lbs.

Overall Length: 85 ft.

Height: 15 ft. 11 in.

Width: 9 ft. 10 in.

Cal-Train bought Bombardier bi-levels to work Baby Bullet express trains between San Francisco and San Jose. A set of bi-levels catches the evening sun at Mountain View, California. *Brian Solomon*

Backlighting on this set of bi-levels on Los Angeles Metrolink at Fullerton clearly shows the older style of riveted construction. *Brian Solomon*

car, which has been an important feature of the design ever since. Hawker-Siddeley affiliate, Can-Car, assumed production in 1988 with the third series of cars. Can-Car was ultimately absorbed by Bombardier, and since the early 2000s, the bi-levels have been built by the multinational railcar manufacturer. The sixth series of cars resulted in a change from riveted to all-welded body construction.

GO Transit wasn't just the first, but also the largest and most extensive user of this bi-level design and has placed orders for all eight series. After GO Transit, the next largest operator has been Los Angeles-area Metrolink, which directly patterned its early 1990s suburban start-up service on GO's successful operations. Other contemporary operators include: Altamont Commuter Express (a limited suburban service running between Stockton and San Jose, California), Cal-Train (San-Francisco-San Jose-Gilroy, California), Coaster (San Diego area suburban service), North Star Commuter Rail (serving Minneapolis, Minnesota), New Mexico's Rail-Runner Express, Sounder commuter rail (Seattle), Sun Rail (Orlando, Florida), Tri-Rail (serving southern Florida), Trinity Railway Express (Dallas-Ft. Worth, Texas), and West Coast Express (centered on Vancouver, British Columbia).

KAWASAKI
RAIL CAR

Since 1991, Kawasaki Rail Car has supplied fleets of bi-level push-pull commuter railcars to Northeastern suburban operators. These fleets have been built to various specifications to comply with the different systems requirements for loading gauge, maximum speed, and seating arrangements. Boston-based MBTA received a fleet of 107 cars designed for 100 miles per hour with 15-foot, 6-inch clearance. Long Island Rail Road operates 134 low-clearance cars with a 14-foot, 5.5-inch clearance, owing to space restrictions in the East River Tunnels on approach to New York's Pennsylvania Station. These are typically worked with EMD DE30AC/DM30AC streamlined diesels (see page 37). Maryland's MARC and Virginia Rail Express commuter systems centered on Washington, DC, bought cars designed for 125 miles per hour top speed.

KAWASAKI COMMUTER CAR SPECIFICATIONS

Type: MBTA Bi-level

Manufacturer: Kawasaki Rail Car

Years Built: Beginning 1991

Seats: A-car 111; B-car 101

Weight: A-car 131,000 lbs., B-car 126,000 lbs.

Overall Length: 85 ft. 4 in.

Height: 15 ft. 6 in.

Width: 10 ft.

Massachusetts Bay Transportation Authority EMD-built F40PH-2C 1070 leads a solid set of Kawasaki bi-level cars along the old Boston & Albany at Auburndale, Massachusetts. *Brian Solomon*

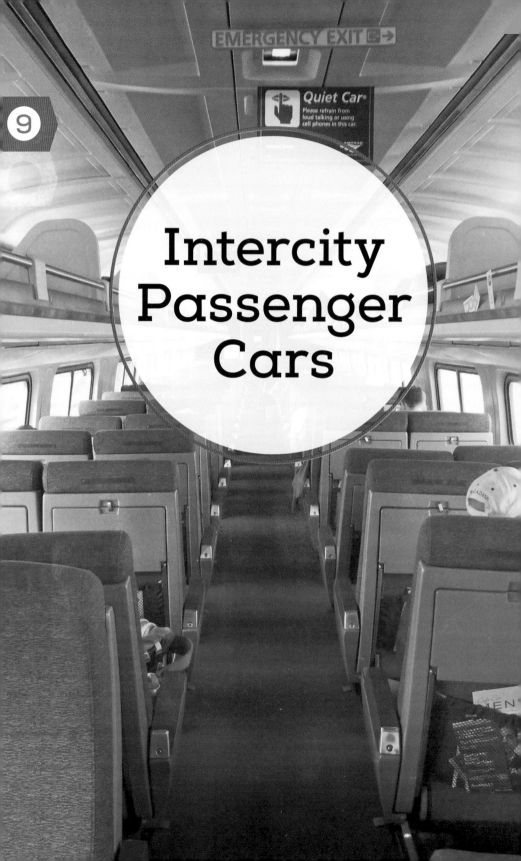

Intercity Passenger Cars

AMFLEET

When Amtrak assumed American intercity passenger services from the private railroads in May 1971, it inherited a rag-tag fleet of postwar streamlined lightweight passenger cars. In 1973, Amtrak decided to order a new fleet of passenger cars patterned after the recently designed Budd *Metroliner* electric multiple-unit cars (originally ordered by the Pennsylvania Railroad).

Like the *Metroliner* cars, the new Budd-built passenger car used a welded stainless-steel tubular design, designed for high-speed (120 miles per hour) operation and intended to withstand high-speed crashes with minimal damage. Amtrak called the new cars Amfleet, and individual configurations were originally designated Amcoach, Amcafe, Amclub, and Amdinette.

Key to success of Amfleet was implementation of the modern Head-end Power system (HEP) concept, where the locomotive generates three-phase alternating current to provide on-board heating, doing away with traditional steam heat and car-mounted electrical generators. Among the cars' other modern features were smaller windows, deemed necessary due to stone-throwing, and disc brakes (requiring a truck-style featuring exposed outer wheel

AMFLEET I SPECIFICATIONS

Type: Corridor service intercity coach

Years Built: 1975-1977

Manufacturer: Budd

Seats: 84

Weight: 106,000 lbs.

Overall Length: 85 ft. 4 in.

Width: NA

OPPOSITE: Amtrak has modernized the interiors of its Amfleet cars. *Brian Solomon*

BELOW: Amfleet 1 car 48176 (originally 20053) was built as an Amcafe and later reconfigured as a Club-Dinette as seen here at Palmer, Massachusetts. *Brian Solomon*

surfaces). An air-suspension system was designed for smooth, quiet ride at high-speed.

Amtrak placed four orders using the initial Amfleet I design, and the last of 492 cars were delivered in June 1977. As built, most conventionally oriented Amcoaches featured eighty-four seats per car, with some cars arranged for long-distance trains featuring just sixty seats to give passengers greater leg room while also making more space for restrooms. The Amcafe has central snack bar with space for fifty-three seats, while the Amclubs feature a central snack bar between twenty-three coach seats on one end of the car and eighteen club seats on the other. Amdinettes have a central snack bar with thirty-two table seats at one end and twenty-three coach seats at the other. This fleet has served as the backbone of Amtrak's eastern corridor services for nearly four decades.

In 1980, Amtrak ordered a revised Amfleet design from Budd, featuring a few minor changes designed for longer-distance services, such as larger windows and fewer seats per car. In 1981, Budd delivered 125 Amfleet II coaches and 25 Amlounges—distinguished by a snack bar with seventeen lounge seats at one end, with thirty-two table seats at the other end. An easy spotting feature for Amfleet IIs are the slightly larger windows, and vestibules and external doors located at only one end of the car (instead of both ends as on Amfleet 1 equipment).

Amfleet 1 82723, seen working train 94 at Richmond, Virginia, is typical of a Coach Class passenger car assigned to Amtrak regional trains working the Northeast Corridor and connecting routes. *Brian Solomon*

SUPERLINERS

Amtrak's Superliner Bi-Level passenger cars have served as the core of its Western long-distance fleet since the 1980s. These amply proportioned cars are also assigned to eastern runs such as the *Capitol Limited* and *Auto Train*, which are not constrained by clearance restrictions on Northeaster lines.

The car's design was patterned on Santa Fe's successful Budd bi-levels introduced in 1956 on its deluxe *El Capitan*. Bi-levels have a variety of advantages, including more capacity and elevated views to better allow passengers to take in the scenery. Amtrak's ordered its first Superliners from Pullman-Standard in 1975. The first car entered service in 1979, and the fleet ultimately totaled 284 cars. These were the very last passenger cars built by the historic manufacturer.

Superliners measure 85 feet long, 10 feet 2 inches wide, and 16 feet 2 inches tall, and the typical car weighs about 157,000 pounds. In place of end vestibules, Superliners feature centrally located doors for boarding. As built, there were several distinct car types: Full Superliner coaches that featured seventy-five seats; Superliner sleepers with fifteen economy bedrooms, five deluxe bedrooms, one family-sized bedroom, and one handicapped bedroom; Dining

SUPERLINER COACH SPECIFICATIONS

Type: High-level intercity passenger car

Years Built: Beginning 1979

Manufacturer: Pullman-Standard

Seats: 75

Weight: 157,000 lbs.

Overall Length: 85 ft.

Height: 16 ft. 2 in.

Width: 10 ft. 2 in.

Amtrak's California Zephyr at Smart Ridge near Emigrant Gap, California, on Donner Pass offers a good vintage perspective on Superliner I equipment in comparison to the slightly smaller former Santa Fe Budd-built high-level cars. *Brian Solomon*

cars with seats for seventy-two diners. In addition, there are Coach-Baggage cars, and I-Lounges known colloquially as "sightseer lounges" that feature prominent glass-covered observation style-roof. In the 1980s, Amtrak reconfigured some Superliners cars.

Amtrak had often assigned the 1950s-era Santa Fe bi-levels to work with Superliners, but these could be easily distinguished by a slightly lower profile and Budd-style stainless steel side-fluting.

In the early 1990s, Amtrak required more long-distance cars, and ordered 140 addition bi-levels, called Superliner IIs from Bombardier, built at its Barre, Vermont, facility. Following the delivery of Superliner IIs in 1993, Amtrak opened up bi-level equipment for services east of Chicago where clearances permitted. Delivery of Superliner IIs roughly coincided with Amtrak's retirement of many older Heritage Fleet cars, including popular types such as the traditional dome cars. Today, most Superliner-equipped long-distance trains use standardized configurations that improve equipment utilization and minimize the need to switch out consists at terminals.

Amtrak Superliner coach/baggage 31035 heading toward Chicago Union Station via the former Alton Route.
Brian Solomon

CALIFORNIA CARS

Amtrak's California corridor services largely employ the custom-designed double-deck California Cars patterned after the Superliners. The design and purchase of these cars were made possible by public ballot initiatives in 1990, which authorized massive public investment in rail expansion. By design, the styling and profile of these cars match the EMD F59PHIs diesels bought to propel them. California Cars were designed for compatibility with other Amtrak equipment and it's common to find Superliners mixed into California Car sets.

In February 1992, California Department of Transportation ordered eighty-eight cars from Morrison-Knudsen to form push-pull sets. However, Morrison-Knudsen was reorganized during production, and the cars were completed by a new company called American Passenger Rail Car Company (known as Amerail), while California scaled back its order to sixty-six cars. This consisted of fourteen 8300-series

CALIFORNIA CAR CAB CONTROL CAR SPECIFICATIONS

Type: Bi-level long-distance Cab Control Car

Years Built: Ordered in 1992 (production delayed)

Manufacturers: Morrison-Knudsen/Amerail

Seats: 86

Weight: 155,000 lbs.

Length: 85 ft.

Height: 16 ft. 1.5 in.

Width: 10 ft. 2.5 in.

Working toward Los Angeles with cab-car first, a *Pacific Surfliner* approaches its station stop at Fullerton, California. *Brian Solomon*

cab-control cars (for operating in push mode using engineer's controls similar to that used on the F59PHI locomotives) with eighty-six passenger seats; thirty-two 8000-series standard coaches with seats for ninety passengers; six 8200 series coach/baggage cars with seats for eighty-four passengers; and fourteen 8800-series food-service cars. Most paid passenger seating is located on the upper level, with toilets and additional seating on the lower level.

In 2000, Amtrak's San Diegan service was re-branded *Pacific Surfliner*. Between 2000 and 2002, Amtrak and California DOT bought cars from Altstom (built in Hornell, New York) to form nine five-car sets for expanded *Pacific Surfliner* service (San Diego-Los Angeles-San Luis Obispo) and other Amtrak California routes. Surfliners are colorfully named after California geographical places, including beaches, canyons, and parks. Eight sets were funded by Amtrak and one by California. In their original configuration, these sets consisted of a 6800-series business class car, two 6400-series coaches, a 6300-series coach/café, and a 6900-series cab car with coach and baggage space. Cars intended for *Pacific Surfliner* service are specially painted in an attractive blue and white livery that emulates the colors of the ocean on a sunny day.

As of 2015, a new-generation of corridor service bi-level cars were on order from Nippon Sharyo, to be constructed in Illinois.

Amtrak styled its California Cars to match the EMD F59PHI diesels ordered at the same time. A westward *Capitols* (Sacramento to San Jose) service rolls along San Pablo Bay at Pinole, California.
Brian Solomon

VIEWLINER

Viewliners were designed by Amtrak as low-level sleeping/dining cars intended for lines with vertical clearance restrictions. Initially, three prototype cars—one diner and two sleepers—were assembled in Indiana at Amtrak's Beech Grove Shops during 1987 and 1988. A Viewliners fleet was anticipated to replace Heritage-fleet cars and has become the primary type of sleeping car on eastern routes that cannot accommodate Superliner equipment. Although cars feature two rows of windows, they are a single-level design, with the upper row of windows providing views from the top bunk in sleeping compartments.

On December 2, 1992, following years of testing, Amtrak finally authorized Morrison-Knudsen to construct fifty Viewliner sleepers (numbers 62000 to 62049). The order was completed in 1995 and 1996 by M-K's railcar building successor, American Passenger Rail Car Company (Amerail).

Viewliner sleeping cars are arranged with twelve standard bedroom compartments, six on each side of

VIEWLINER SLEEPER SPECIFICATIONS

Type: Single-level sleeping car

Years Built: 1995-1996

Manufacturers: Morrison-Knudsen/Amerail

Seats: Bedrooms: 12 standard, 2 deluxe, and 1 handicapped accessible

Weight: 140,500 lbs.

Overall Length: 85 ft. 4 in.

Height: 14 ft.

Width: 10 ft. 6 in.

On May 9, 2015, Amtrak 449, the Boston-Chicago section of the *Lake Shore Limited*, carried a brand-new, CAF-built Viewliner 2 baggage car on the head end. *Brian Solomon*

the car, plus two deluxe bedrooms, and a handicapped bedroom. Standard bedrooms are designed to accommodate two passengers with two facing seats and central retractable table. At night, the seats convert into a lower bunk, and an upper bunk can be lowered into place. Standard bedrooms feature a sink and non-enclosed toilet, while additional toilet facilities are located at the end of the car.

As built, each sleeper carries a name ending in "View," with the first in the series being the American View. Viewliner sleepers are routinely assigned to the following eastern long-distance trains: New York-Florida trains *Silver Star* and *Silver Meteor*, both Boston and New York sections of the *Lake Shore Limited* (although, depending on the availability of cars the Boston section may run without its dedicated sleeping car), tri-weekly New York-Washington DC-Chicago *Cardinal*, and New York to New Orleans *Crescent*. In the early days of Viewliner operation, they also served the Boston-New York-Washington DC-Newport News, *Twilight Shoreliner*.

A vintage General Electric center cab switcher shifts the brand-new Viewliner 2 sleeper, *Portage River*. Spain's Construcciones y Auxiliar de Ferrocarriles, S.A. (CAF) builds cars for the US market in Elmira, New York. *Tim Doherty*

TALGO

TALGO is a Spanish railway manufacturer with ties to American railroads dating back to the 1940s. TALGO passenger car bodies are famous for their lightweight low-profile tubular designs that are coupled with fixed articulated sets that straddle a common set of wheels. One of their most unusual features is that rather than trucks, TALGO employs independent wheel pairs that do not share a common axle. In the 1950s, Boston & Maine, New Haven, and Rock Island experimented with TALGOs, and Amtrak tested one in 1988.

In 1994-1995, Amtrak imported twelve- and fourteen-car TALGO TP-200 trains for testing in the Pacific Northwest and elsewhere. Modern TALGO designs use a tilting system for better passenger comfort in curves. Amtrak and Washington state cooperated in an order for four TALGO Series VI sets to expand regional *Cascades* service between Eugene, Seattle, and Vancouver, BC These were delivered in 1998 and feature an unusual exterior design with large fiberglass fins to provide a better visual transition between F59PHI diesels and the low-profile cars. Oregon bought a pair of thirteen-car Series 8 TALGO trains that were delivered in 2013. In 2009, the state of Wisconsin ordered 110-miles-per-hour Series 8 trains. These were built in Milwaukee, but political changes resulted in the state canceling the order before they turned a wheel.

TALGO SERIES VIII SPECIFICATIONS

Type: Intercity tilting articulated trains

Years Built: 2013

Manufacturer: Renfe-Talgo of America

Wheel Arrangement: Articulated 13-car set

Seats: 250 per 13 car train

Weight: NA

Overall Length: 43.1 ft. (intermediate car)

Height: 13.1 ft.

Width: 9.65 ft.

Amtrak's *Cascades* tilting TALGO trains feature large fiberglass fins designed to allow a visual transition between EMD F59PHI diesels and these unusually low profile cars. *Scott Lothes*

VIA RAIL LRC

VIA Rail, Canada's national intercity passenger train operator, began in 1977 as a subsidy of Canadian National Railways, and one year later assumed operation of both CN and Canadian Pacific's intercity passenger services, serving a role comparable to Amtrak in the United States. Initially, it used equipment inherited from CN and CP. Between 1981 and 1984, it took delivery of its first large order for new passenger equipment, consisting of recently designed Light Rapid Comfortable (LRC) cars and engines built by Bombardier. The passenger cars use an active tilting mechanism to reduce the effects of centrifugal forces on passengers when traveling through curves, thus permitting higher operating speeds on sinuous routes. Specialized model M429LRC locomotives with wedge-shaped front ends were built as LRC power cars, but all were withdrawn by 2001. Today, LRC trains are led by F40PH-2D or GE P42DC diesels.

VIA Rail's LRC fleet consists of seventy-two LRC Coaches (numbers 3300 to 3399) and twenty-four LRC Club cars (3451 to 3475). Both types feature spacious passenger accommodation with large picture windows and airline style overhead luggage storage. Additional space for baggage is located in a vestibule at one end of the car, with toilets at the far end. Coaches feature sixty-eight seats per car; club cars, fifty-four seats per car.

LRC CLUB CAR SPECIFICATIONS

Type: First-class long-distance tilting coach

Years Built: 1984

Manufacturer: Bombardier

Seats: 54

Weight: NA

Overall Length: NA

Height: NA

Width: NA

In May 1985, a VIA Rail LRC train roars west on the Canadian National at Dorval, Quebec. *Brian Solomon*

VIA Rail's 1980s-vintage LRC passenger cars use a low-profile design that is substantially shorter than the General Electric Genesis diesels now used to haul them on corridor services among Quebec City, Montreal, Toronto, and Windsor, Ontario. *Brian Solomon*

Freight Cars

BOXCARS

Historically, the boxcar was the universal conveyor of railroad freight, used to carry just about every type of cargo. The car's simplicity and exceptional versatility made it desirable by shippers and carriers for hauling everything from machinery to harvested grain. However, as railroads evolved into more specialized movers of freight, their freight car requirements changed; today, special service cars dominate, and while they are less versatile, they are also better suited to the peculiarities of different types of traffic.

While it could be used to haul a great variety of cargo, one of the boxcar's failings was its inefficiency in loading, unloading, and using the space efficiently. The rapid rise of intermodal shipping and unit trains coincided with both the steep decline in the number of boxcars and the cars' relative percentage of the total fleet. In 1954, Pennsylvania Railroad, which operated one of the largest fleets of freight cars, rostered more than 66,000 boxcars, accounting for nearly 36 percent of its entire fleet. That's a greater number of cars than CSX had in 2012 of all types. In 1980, before the effects of deregulation transformed railroad shipping,

This new FBOX is an example of 50-foot plug-door High Cube boxcar with the taller than average profile designated it as a Plate F car. *Brian Solomon*

OPPOSITE: Kansas City Southern covered hoppers. *Brian Solomon*

American railroads had more than 251,000 plain boxcars and another 179,000 insulated or specially equipped cars. Thirty years later, these totals were just 12,078 and 83,436 respectively. In 1984, boxcars of various types (excluding mechanical refrigerator cars for perishable traffic) represented more than 20 percent of the American fleet, while twenty-five years later these cars were barely more than 8 percent of the total.

The size of the individual boxcar has grown. The old wooden cars of the nineteenth century would seem tiny by modern standards; by the 1930s, the standard-size car was the 40-foot, 50-ton boxcar. A classic example of this type was PRR's X29, built by the thousands between 1924 and 1934. Gradually, railroads upped the standard size of cars. By the mid-1980s, the old 40-foot cars were rapidly vanishing from interchange service. Today, the fleets of once-common 50-foot cars are thinning and will soon be gone. Yet, for some services, 40- and 50-foot hi-cube (tall-profile plate F car) cars remain as a desired type. Other common car lengths are those measuring 52, 60, 62, and 70 feet. Expansive 86-foot cars, once used for auto-parts service, were the largest standard boxcar type, but these have fallen out of favor and are no longer being built.

Pan Am Railways 50-foot boxcars roll along Canadian Pacific's former Delaware & Hudson carrying paper products from Maine. *Brian Solomon*

RAILCAR MARKINGS

Key markings on the sides and ends of railcars describe the ownership, loading dimensions, and weight characteristics, as well as braking information and other specific equipment on the railcar. Railcars capable of carrying hazardous materials have spaces for standardized hazmat warning placards.

All railcars are identified by reporting marks and car numbers. A reporting mark is an alphabetic code of two to four letters used to identify owners or lessees of rolling stock and other equipment. Combined with the car number, this gives the railcar its unique ID. The letter codes are assigned to railroads and private railcar owners by the American Association of Railroads' (AAR) subsidiary Railinc. Typically, the letter codes are derived from

the railroad name; historically, New York Central was NYC, Pennsylvania Railroad was PRR, etc. Private car owners have reporting marks that end in the letter X. Thousands of different reporting marks are in use today, often with railroads assigning car fleets to various affiliates or subsidiary companies. The reporting marks significantly tell the true owner of the car and not the name painted on the side. As a result, it is common to find freight cars still operating with the names of long-merged railroads painted on the sides, but with contemporary reporting marks.

Dimensional information includes the load limit, indicated by LD LMT, and the railcar's empty tare weight (light weight), indicated by LT WT— both are followed by a total weight figure given in pounds. The overall dimensions of the car are indicated by a plate figure shown in a black box. Standard plate dimensions are plates B, C, E, and F, G, H. These dimensions describe a railcar's profile. In addition, specific dimensions are indicated in feet and inches as follows: EXW describes the extreme width of the car; EW is the width over the eaves of the railcar; IL is the interior length; IW the interior width; and IH is interior height; and cubic feet, with initials CF (for example: 4750cf), describes overall car volume.

The railcar's original construction date is indicated by BLT followed by numbers reflecting month and year, such as 12-08. If the car was rebuilt, the initials REBLT are followed by a similar date indication. Tank cars will have descriptions of maximum capacity in gallons and liters, details on safety valves, and maximum tank pressure in pounds per square inch.

Diamond-shaped placard holders are used for standardized United States Department of Transportation hazardous materials placards. These are only inserted when hazardous materials may be encountered (which occurs in some cases even when the load has been discharged, because residual materials may remain in the car). Standard placards are: Class 1 (orange) for explosives; Class 2, compressed gases; Class 3, flammable liquids; Class 4, flammable solids; Class 5, oxidizers; Class 6, poisons; Class 7, radioactive materials; Class 8, corrosive liquids; and Class 9, miscellaneous. The class number is located at the bottom of the card.

OPEN HOPPERS

Since the nineteenth century, open hoppers have been a staple railcar used for moving bulk cargo unaffected by exposure to the elements, such as coal and aggregates. Coal hoppers are one of North America's most common railcars, having grown from small two bay railcars to large high-capacity multiple bay units. On traditional coal-hauling lines, vast numbers of hoppers were on the move at any one time. In 1910, the Lackawanna originated as many as one thousand loaded hoppers daily from Anthracite mines around Scranton, dispatching them in trains of forty to fifty railcars. In the 1940s, Chesapeake & Ohio, a line that built its fortunes on the movement of bituminous coal, was moving 160-car trains from its sprawling classification yards at Clifton Forge east to its coal piers at Newport News, and west Lake Erie Maumee Bay near Toledo, Ohio, where in 1942, its massive Presque Isle Docks handled an average of 2,150 cars daily, emptying a hopper car into waiting lake boats every 45 seconds.

Pennsylvania Railroad had one of the largest fleets of open hoppers, which in the mid-1950s consisted of more than seventy thousand cars. Almost half its fleet were variations of its H2a, which had a steel 70-ton three-bay typical of a mid-twentieth century coal car.

Southern Railway pioneered the unit coal train concept. In the late 1950s and early 1960s, it devised an arrangement to use a fleet of new large-capacity aluminum hoppers designed for rapid loading and rapid discharge. These were operated in dedicated lines directly from the mines to the power plant, which dramatically improved railcar utilization.

Coal hoppers cost more than gondolas, but they can discharge faster and don't require expensive rotary dumping equipment, and are therefore often preferred for relatively short runs. By the mid-2000s, North American coal-hauling fleets were in roughly even balance between rotary gondolas and bottom-discharge hopper cars. In recent year, eastern utilities converting to Powder River coal largely have favored the acquisition of rapid-discharge bottom dump-cars with interconnected hatches typically opened and closed using electro-pneumatic controls. Today, most coal is moved by dedicated unit trains of 105 cars or more.

This Pennsylvania Power & Light (PPLX) car 1094 is a hundred-ton, three-bay steel hopper built by Bethlehem Steel Corporation in July, 1976. This car features rotary couplers that allow the car to remain coupled in a train-set when rotated into a car dumper.
Pat Yough

COVERED HOPPERS

By the early 1990s, the covered hopper had emerged
as North America's most prolific class of freight car,
representing more than 25 percent of the fleet. This basic
type has two principal variations identified by how they
are unloaded: traditional gravity discharge or pneumatic
discharge. The gravity car remains the more common
variety. Pneumatic cars can be subdivided into those
operated with a vacuum versus those using positive
pressure. Pressurized cars both aid with the unloading
process and help prevent cargo contamination. Cars can be
further categorized depending on the number of bays or
compartments, total capacity by weight, the type of loading
equipment, and steel versus aluminum construction.

Covered hoppers are widely used as grain cars, but
also carry a variety of heavy bulk commodities such as
cement, fertilizer, phosphate, silica, sugar, malt, plastic
pellets, and potash, that would be damaged by exposure
to the elements. Many sub-varieties of covered hopper
are traffic-specific designs. Cement is typically carried
in relatively short, two-bay hoppers—a design with less
voluminous bays suitable to the greater density and
weight of cement compared to other types of cargo. A
typical cement hopper is a relatively compact (Plate B) car

ABOVE: Typical of Canadian government grain cars are these cylindrical Alberta Grain cars owned by the province of Alberta. *Brian Solomon*

LEFT: Southern Railway's Big John aluminum hoppers were of an innovative high-capacity design that in the 1960s helped establish the covered hopper as the new standard for grain shipments. *Brian Solomon*

measuring just 41 feet 11 inches long, while a hopper used for grain and other lighter cargo would feature three or four bays and measure 59 feet long. Less common is the highly specialized cylindrical, low-slung pressurized cement hopper.

Historically, grain was transported in boxcars, so one of the most important developments in rail freight transport in the mid-twentieth century occurred in 1960, when Southern Railway revolutionized grain transport with the introduction of high volume, four-compartment aluminum-covered hoppers that it called *Big Johns*. The first batch of cars had a 97-ton capacity, but the capacity was incrementally increased so by the mid-1960s Southern was operating 130-ton grain hoppers. Today, grain hoppers are standard equipment.

A common type used on Canadian lines are Government grain cars. These are typically 100-ton cars with four bays, offering 4,550 cubic feet capacity. Cars are variously administered by the Grain Transportation Agency, Canadian Wheat Board, and governments of Alberta and Saskatchewan. Among the classic paint schemes are red body cars with large yellow grain silhouettes with "Canada" painted in large white letters and the maple leaf insignia on the sides.

Kansas City Southern operates a large fleet of these attractively painted three-bay covered hoppers. *Brian Solomon*

INTERMODAL
FLATS AND WELL CARS

Trailer Train (renamed TTX Company in 1991), was an outgrowth of Pennsylvania Railroad's interest in piggyback/intermodal operations and has played a fundamental role in the design, growth, and management of intermodal cars in North America. The company was originally jointly owned by PRR, N&W, and General Motors' affiliate Rail Trailer. Eventually, other major railroads bought shares and TTX was transformed into an industry-wide intermodal equipment pool supply. Its individual railcars can be loaded by any member railroad (or nonmembers with a member's permission), which allows for more efficient railcar utilization. Because it controlled a nationwide pool, Trailer Train was in a position to establish industry-wide intermodal railcar standards. For example, in 1958, TTX introduced the trailer hitch as standard equipment. This was a clever innovation that eliminated securing-chains and other clumsy tie-down equipment while providing an effective cushioning device and greatly simplifying piggyback loading.

In 1952, Electro-Motive Division designed a specialized prototype, low-tare weight 75-foot flatcar designed to carry a pair of 35-foot highway trailers; it was specially designed to both speed and simplify the trailer loading process. Trailer Train bought five hundred specially designed piggyback flatcars derived from this prototype. But no sooner were these cars in service than the trucking industry introduced higher-capacity, 40-foot long trailers. The 75-foot flat was obsolete from the moment it was built, and as a result Trailer Train adopted the 85-foot trailer flat car as its new standard in 1958. This proved to be a versatile and useful intermodal vehicle that could accommodate two standard 40-foot highway trailers or three shorter "pup" trailers that were popular some trucking companies.

In the 1960s, TTX introduced the 89-foot 4-inch flat car as its latest standard, but the older 85-foot flat cars remained in service for decades. In later years these were reassigned to specialized services, such as transporting long poles and metal pipe. A typical Trailer Train 89-foot TTX for

trailer-on-flatcar service weighed 68,000 pounds; while the trailer-carrying portion of the car measured 89 feet 4 inches long, and its full length was 92 feet 8 inches long over coupler faces, with a platform 9 feet wide. As built, the flat car had a pair of retractable trailer hitches and a pair of bridge plates to drive trailers from one flat car to another.

This TTX three-unit articulated car was built by Gunderson. It is designed to move 53-foot domestic containers and is typical of modern 125-ton intermodal cars. *Brian Solomon*

In the mid-1970s, Santa Fe pioneered the design of lightweight articulated flatcars. A six-unit prototype car known as the *six pack* made its debut in 1976, and the concept was soon expanded into a ten-unit car variously known as *ten-pack* or the *Fuel Foiler*. Instead of traditional flat-car construction, these modern railcars feature a spine design, where a central sill bridges between truck centers and supports strategically placed platform sections to carry trailer wheels. Tare weight was lowered by the use of drawbar connections instead of conventional couplers, which also reduced slack between units. Santa Fe licensed production of the Fuel Foiler to Itel Rail Division. Various spine car configurations have developed, and it has become a dominant type of single-level intermodal flat.

Southern Pacific spawned a key innovation in 1977 when, working with ACF, it designed a prototype double-stack container car. This type featured bulkheads at each end to secure and support a 40-foot container stacked upon another that was positioned in the railcar well. In 1981, SP was the first railroad to order production of double-stack cars, which foreshadowed a revolution in intermodal transport.

Gunderson designed another bulkhead style stack car called the Twin-Stack. This was developed in the

Conrail's TV305 snakes through the Canisteo River Valley on March 23, 1988. The train is largely Thrall-built five-unit articulated stack wells carrying steamship containers for American President Lines. *Brian Solomon*

mid-1980s, initially as a five-unit articulated set that offered ten container platforms: with two 20-foot or one 40-foot container on the lower level, while adjustable bulkheads could accommodate 40-, 45-, or 48-foot containers on the upper level. By 1988, 4,160 Twin-Stacks were in service. However, owing to the limitations of the bulkhead design, this type fell out of favor.

Gunderson's Maxi-Stack did away with bulkheads. This type of railcar underwent several significant design and production phases. The Maxi-Stack III entered production in 1989, designed to transport 20- to 48-foot containers in the well, with 40- to 53-foot containers stacked on top. It became the dominant type of double-stack car. Another variation is the Maxi-Stack IV, a three-unit articulated well car designed to handle pairs of 20-foot containers, and single containers 40 to 53 feet long. Gunderson's standalone (non-articulated) Husky-Stack and AP53 "All Purpose Double-Stack Car" was specifically built for 53-foot domestic containers. (The AP53 was also sold in three-unit articulated sets.)

Another early type of stack car began as the Budd-designed Lo-Pac articulated car, which used a floorless drop-frame arrangement without requiring bulkheads to support the stacked container. Instead, this employed an interbox connector (similar to that used on ships) to secure containers by locking top containers to the bottom ones. Eliminating bulkheads allowed for a light-weight railcar with a simple design.

CSX Intermodal 53-foot containers glide along on TTAX 53 all-purpose spine cars. *Brian Solomon*

AUTORACKS

An autorack is a common type of specialized flatcar. It began in the late-1950s as an adaptation of the intermodal flat, and many were built using the standard TTX flat fitted with bi-level and tri-level automobile carrying rack structures (thus leading to the cars' commonly being referred to as *multilevels* or *autoracks*). Widespread adoption of these autoracks by the North American railroad industry enabled it to increase its market share of new automotive traffic from 10 percent in the 1950s to roughly 70 percent by the mid-1990s. In 1981, major American railroads began a system-wide car-pooling arrangement to obtain better autorack utilization and to streamline operations by minimizing empty railcar movements. Also in the 1980s, the AAR implemented standardized specifications for both bi-level and tri-level cars.

The fleet has gradually evolved from open cars to modern fully enclosed autoracks with adjustable mid-level platforms. The old open autoracks allowed great views of new automobiles rolling by on trains; unfortunately these did little to protect their high-value cargo from vandalism

This TTX pool car seen passing Covington, Kentucky on CSX carries BTTX reporting marks. It is standard 140-foot bi-level articulated autorack built by Thrall. *Brian Solomon*

or damage while in transit. Partially enclosed autoracks began entering the pool in 1982. Since then, fully enclosed cars with galvanized side-panels and roofs and secured end-doors have become standard in North America. In the mid-1990s, AAR revised the screen hole pattern on the side panels reducing the amount of open space to just 4 to 6 percent in order to better protect new automobiles. Another change was improved mainline clearances, which by the late-1990s had allowed for maximum autorack height to increase from 19 feet to 20 feet 2 inches.

A modern autorack variation is the two-section articulated design using three sets of two-axle trucks, typically measuring 140 feet long with 58 feet between truck centers. In the late 1990s, Greenbrier's Gunderson introduced its 20-foot 2-inch Auto-Max car. Its more advanced Auto-Max II is a 145-foot long articulated car with depressed center sections and adjustable mid-levels that provide the most capacity of any commercially-built autorack and can accommodate up to twenty SUVs on three levels. Similar is Gunderson's non-articulated Multi-Max car, introduced in 2013, that features a high-capacity design with adjustable mid-levels. Single-level enclosed autoracks are less common than multi-levels; these are used to move small trucks, school buses, and farm equipment.

This TTX pool TTGX car is an example of a Greenbrier Multi-Max autorack with adjustable mid-level decks. *Brian Solomon*

TANK CARS

The North American railroad tank car has its origins as a vehicle for bulk petroleum transport dating from the 1860s, and while the railcar type has undergone a variety of transformations in the last century and a half, it remains an important means of moving petroleum products and other liquid commodities. Since the early 1900s, there has been a high level of scrutiny and more intense regulation regarding the design and operation of tank cars owing to the flammable, toxic, or otherwise hazardous nature of many cargos. There are more than one hundred types of liquids carried by tank cars, including industrial chemicals, acids, and fuels, but also less hazardous materials such as corn syrup and vegetable oil. Railroads have also used tank cars to move water both to supply steam locomotives at remote, arid locations and on fire-protection trains.

A typical tank car consists of a tank shell with tank heads at the ends and top and/or bottom valves for loading and unloading, along with pressure-relief valves. Most tank cars are insulated, and many types of non-pressurized tank cars are equipped with heater coils. Cars designed to carry flammable cargo service must have reinforced metal at the ends, called head shields.

One of the heaviest trains on Southern Pacific in the early 1990s was its BKDOL (Bakersfield to Dolores Yard, California) unit train known colloquially as the Oil Cans. *Brian Solomon*

Periodic revisions to tank car regulations has occurred, usually in response to serious accidents involving flammable or other hazardous cargo. In the last decade, railroads have experienced a rapid growth in ethanol and crude oil traffic, increasing the demand for tank cars. Several high-profile disasters have prompted recent revisions to cars used in High-hazard flammable trains (known as HHFT, these are defined as twenty or more tank cars loaded with flammable liquid or thirty-five or more cars so loaded spread throughout a train). In May 2015, the AAR, Hazardous Materials Safety Administration, and Federal Railroad Administration, along with the Canadian Transportation Ministry introduced new regulations for the production and operation of HHFT tank cars. These include changes to construction specifications for tank cars after October 1, 2015, and a schedule mandating the retrofitting of existing tank cars to bring them up to modern safety standards. HHFT trains will be limited to 50 miles per hour, and tank car design has been modified to included full-height, half-inch-thick head shields, thicker tank shells, and a ceramic thermal shield. An improved bottom valve design must be implemented to prevent a car from accidentally discharging its load in a derailment or crash.

Many tank cars are purchased for a specific type of traffic. This PLMX tank is designated to carry molten sulfur. *Brian Solomon*

PART 4
Rail Transit

INTRODUCTION

Electric street railways made their debut in the 1880s. These were among the earliest commercial applications for electricity, and in the late nineteenth and early twentieth centuries, before the predominance of automobiles, electric railway cars provided local transport in cities and towns all across North America, while lightly built electric "interurbans" connected a vast territory as well. Early trolley cars were built by a variety of manufacturers with some common patterns and numerous variations. Colorful bouncing trolley cars were adapted from horse cars, which had evolved from the horse-drawn omnibus. In the twentieth century, double-truck cars replaced the old four-wheel cars, and wooden bodies gave way to steel. Cars grew in size and shape.

By the 1920s, automobiles and buses were eroding streetcar traffic. In the mid-1930s, the Electric Railway Presidents' Conference Committee Car (PCC car) was developed to combat declining streetcar traffic. This technologically advanced streetcar featuring an automotive-inspired streamlined design entered production in 1936, rapidly becoming the most common North American streetcar (see Chapter 6). Despite this, the decline continued and accelerated after World War II. By the 1960s, most cities had abandoned streetcars (and many cities began to suffer from urban blight as well). A few systems survived, often where old streetcar lines were blended with faster modes of urban transit, benefitting from private rights-of-way, elevated structures, or streetcar subways. PCC cars (see page 193) continued to work in Boston, Newark, New Jersey, Pittsburgh, Philadelphia, Cleveland,

Houston's MetroRail is one of several modern light-rail systems that favors Siemens S70 cars. Cars stop at Fannin Street. *Tom Kline*

PREVIOUS PAGE: Los Angeles Metro operates Breda LRVs on its Gold Line. *Brian Solomon*

San Diego Trolley began service in 1981 using a fleet of Siemens-Dueweg U2 cars. *Brian Solomon*

and San Francisco into the early 1980s. By this time, the tide had begun to turn as funding became available, and new trolleys were ordered—although now they weren't called trolleys, but rather *light rail vehicles*. Since all the traditional America streetcar builders had exited the business, in the late 1970s Boston and San Francisco bought articulated LRVs from Boeing-Vertol. In 1980, Philadelphia ordered cars from Japanese manufacturer Kawasaki, while Cleveland bought cars from Breda, and Pittsburgh invested in Siemens cars while morphing its streetcar network into a more modern light rail system.

About the same time, a North American light rail revival was sparked with the opening of Edmonton, Alberta's all-new

system in 1978. And the opening of the San Diego Trolley in 1981 got the ball rolling in the United States. San Diego rediscovered the virtues of electric streetcars as a means of providing cost effective rail-based transport over a lightly used freight lines in the city. Even so, by the 1970s most American cities had abandoned traditional streetcar services. Only a handful of cities, such as San Francisco, Boston, and Philadelphia, still retained portions of their old streetcar networks. Although today most of these electrically-operated networks are known as light rail systems, they embrace many of the essential qualities of older electric street railways. By the 1990s, a variety of North American cities were building light rail or contemplating it.

A set of Siemens SD100 cars work the Draper Line on the Utah Transit Authority's TRAX light rail against a backdrop of snow-crested peaks. *Jack May*

was the reinvention of the streetcar. While a minor distinction, a modern streetcar system can be defined as a line that uses mostly street running, doesn't require complicated platforms to board cars, and uses lightweight low-floor designs.

Among the early cities to embrace the light rail revolution were Buffalo, New York; St. Louis, Missouri; Denver, Colorado; Baltimore, Maryland; and Portland, Oregon. By 2015, the list of cities with light rail and modern streetcar systems is pretty impressive, now including Seattle and Tacoma, Washington; Charlotte, North Carolina; Minneapolis–St. Paul, Minnesota; Norfolk, Virginia; Salt Lake City, Utah; Phoenix and Tucson, Arizona; Dallas and Houston, Texas; and New Jersey's Hudson waterfront cities focused on Jersey City and Hoboken. Additional systems are underway in Washington, DC, Atlanta, and Cincinnati, among other cities.

Light Rail cars have been supplied by international railcar builders, including Bombardier, Breda, Kawasaki, Kinkisharyo, Nippon Sharyo, Siemens, and Skoda. In some instances, cars have been custom designed, but often cities opt for standard designs or adapt established light rail car types without extensive new engineering.

Rapid transit systems are specialized passenger railways that tend to embrace a set of characteristics that distinguish them from both light rail and heavy rail networks. In general, rapid transit networks use fully electrified, isolated, and largely grade-separated routes that often involve a heavily engineered infrastructure including deep tunnels, subways, cuttings, and extensive elevated structures. In most instances, stations involve some variety of positive fare protection (turnstiles or barriers) and loading is via high-level platforms. The isolated nature of the systems allows for customized car fleets with non-standard loading gauge specifications. The cars tend to be lower and lighter than mainline heavy railcars, and are often designed to work line profiles that have significantly steeper grades and sharper curves than is practical on conventional heavy rail lines. Closed and isolated operations with customized equipment have also allowed for use of advanced signaling and propulsion systems, as well as the occasional novel or peculiar trackage arrangements, including guided rubber tire lines, mono-rail, and elevated suspended tracks. Lighter cars, electric propulsion, advanced signaling, and exclusive rights of way permits rapid acceleration and unusually tight spacing between trains.

In some instances, rapid transit systems share operating characteristics and similar equipment employed by advanced light rail systems. In these situations the primary distinguishing characteristic of rapid transit may be its entirely exclusive right of way. In terms of historical development, where light rail can trace its development to the horse-drawn omnibus and horse cars, rapid transit cars are generally derived from heavy rail designs.

Using a fleet of 1,356 cars, Chicago Transit Authority operates an intensive rapid transit service on 224 track miles using a mix of historic L and subway routes. A set of CTA's Boeing-Vertol 2400-series cars work the downtown Loop. *Brian Solomon*

Light Rail

SIEMENS
LIGHT RAIL

Siemens has been one of the most prolific producers of light rail vehicles for the North America market, with its cars now working in seventeen American cities. Significantly, it played a key role in the light rail revival that began with the opening of the Edmonton, Alberta, system in 1978, and gained momentum with the debut in 1981 of the San Diego Trolley and the Calgary, Alberta, light rail systems. All used Siemens-Duewag U2 cars. Later advancements of the U2 design include the boxy-looking U2A cars as used in Sacramento; similar-looking SD100/SD160 cars bought by Denver, Salt Lake City, and San Diego (SD100 only), among other cities; and SD400 cars used in St. Louis-area Bi-State Transit and Pittsburgh-area Port Authority of Allegheny County. Portland's Tri-Met bought SD660 cars.

Siemens' S70 is a family of low-floor cars formulated specifically for the North American market. Using a modular format, the S70 type can be tailored to an individual transit system's requirements without substantial design changes.

Utah Transit Authority's first cars were Siemens-Duewag SD100s built in 1998. Similar-looking SD160 cars came in 2004—the primary technical difference is the SD160s use modern AC traction motors, while the SD100s are powered by traditional DC motors. At the center of this line is SD100 car 1001, with SD160s on either side of it. *Jack May*

OPPOSITE: The *Lynx* of Charlotte, North Carolina, uses Siemens S70 light rail cars. *Brian Solomon*

Portland's MAX light-rail network began operations in 1986. In 1998 and 2004, it bought fleets of Siemens SD660 light-rail cars (201 to 252 and 301 to 327), such as this one seen at Portland Union Station. *Jack May*

Cars use an articulated design, typically with three sections, and range from 91 to 96 feet long. These can be arranged for either light rail or streetcar style operations. Among the buyers of S70s has been Norfolk, Virginia's Tide, which bought nine double-ended all-low-floor cars 93.6 feet long. These have a maximum speed of 66 miles per hour (limited in service to 55 miles per hour) and 68 seats per car. Portland Tri-Met has ordered fleets of S70 Max cars that feature a sleeker exterior design. Charlotte's Lynx light rail began service with S70s in 2007. San Diego and Houston also operate fleets of S70 cars.

In 2014, San Francisco Muni placed a large order with Siemens for S200 cars. These have a maximum design speed of 55 miles per hour, but limited to 50 miles per hour in service. They use a mix of high- and low-floors. Owing to the steep gradients on Muni's system these will be capable of ascending grades up to 9 percent. Siemens constructs its modern light rail cars at its Sacramento, California, railcar plant.

San Diego, which began with Siemens-Dueweg U2 cars in 1981, has continued to purchase Siemens light rail cars, including a fleet of SD100 cars such as those pictured. *Brian Solomon*

SEPTA'S KAWASAKI
LIGHT RAIL CARS

In 1980, Philadelphia-centered South Eastern Pennsylvania Transportation Authority ordered of two fleets of Kawasaki light rail cars. This includes 112 single-ended cars with fifty-one seats (9000 to 9111), bought for former Philadelphia Transit Company's surface-subway routes (numbers 10, 11, 13, 34, 36). These routes run below ground in the historic Center City subway featuring low-level platforms and continue onto the surface for street running. These cars replaced former PTC PCC cars. A pair of trial cars were tested prior to construction of the remainder of the fleet. Cars entered service in 1981-1982.

SEPTA operates two distinct fleets of Kawasaki light rail vehicle. The double-ended cars work former Red Arrow lines and feature pantographs.
Brian Solomon

Similar are SEPTA's twenty-nine double-ended Kawasaki cars, which are slightly longer with fifty seats per car. They operate on former Philadelphia Suburban Transportation Company/Red Arrow routes running from the 69th Street Terminal (at the terminus of the Market St rapid transit el) in Upper Darby to Media and Sharon Hill, Pennsylvania. These lines feature a mix of private right-of-way and street running. The cars replaced a truly antique fleet of Brill streetcars that were some of the last traditional non-PCC cars remaining in regular revenue service in the United States.

SEPTA's single-ended Kawasaki cars collect current from overhead wire using traditional trolley poles.
Brian Solomon

SKODA

Skoda is a Czech firm with a long history manufacturing railway vehicles including trams and locomotives. It offers a variety of modern low-floor modular articulated trams/light rail vehicles. These range from its model 3T, a single-ended three-section four-axle car measuring 69 feet 5 inches long, to its 19T, a double-ended five-section six-axle car just over 101 feet 8.5 inches long. Its cars are powered using an efficient microprocessor controlled three-phase AC traction system that converts overhead direct current to modulated AC for asynchronous traction motors.

Portland and Tacoma imported Skoda cars for use on their modern streetcar systems. (The system is loosely distinguished from light rail by predominant street running where rail vehicles mix with road traffic, with nominally lighter rail cars with simpler passenger stations.)

Portland's first batch of ten three-section streetcars was built by the now-dissolved Skoda-Inekon partnership in Plzen, Czech Republic. Since the first of these car entered service in 2001, Skoda licensed its Astra 10T design to United Streetcar for domestic production in the United States at Clackamas, Oregon. Skoda has sold its cars for use on various Czech transit systems, as well as elsewhere in Europe, Russia, and China.

Portland's first batch of three-section streetcars (as distinct from its larger light-rail cars) were Astra 10Ts built by the Skoda-Inekon consortium.
Jack May

BREDA
LIGHT RAIL
VEHICLES

The Italian manufacturing firm AnsaldoBreda was formed in 2001 by the merger of Ansaldo Transporti and Breda Costruzioni Ferroviarie. Breda has had a long history in designing and manufacturing trams and light rail vehicles, and its sales of equipment to American transit systems straddled its corporate transition. Since the early 1980s, four cities in the United States have bought and operated Breda cars. While there are family similarities between these cars, they vary in size, weight, and seating specifications as required by their individual systems and feature different propulsion systems as a result of advances in electrical technology.

Cleveland's Regional Transit Authority was first to invest in Breda LRVs, receiving forty-eight two-section articulated cars (numbers 801 to 848) in 1980 and 1981 to replace its aged fleet of PCC cars. These are boxy-looking high-floor cars with bodies made from rust-resistant Corten steel with stainless steel outsides, and are powered by a full chopper propulsion system designed with acceleration and braking characteristics similar to those of heavy-rail metro cars.

Boston's Breda-built Type 8s have two powered trucks and one unpowered truck.
Brian Solomon

Boston-based Massachusetts Bay Transportation Authority assembled a fleet of ninety-five articulated six-axle cars between 1999 and 2007 to augment its fleet of Kinki Sharyo LRVs and allow retirement of remaining 1970s-era Boeing-Vertol cars used on its Green Line light rail routes and trolley subway. MBTA designates these as its Type 8s, which follows logically after the Kinki-Sharyo type 7s. The Breda Type 8s feature high-floor sections at car ends and a low-floor section in the center of the car. Maximum speed is 55 miles per hour.

San Francisco Muni acquired a fleet of 151 Breda LRVs (numbers 1400 to 1551) for service on its light rail and Muni Metro routes to supplant its Boeing-Vertol cars (similar to Boston's). The first fifty Breda cars were ordered in late 1991, and deliveries began in 1995. The cars were shipped cross-country on flatcars, many crossing Donner Pass on their way West. Cars draw current from 600 volt DC overhead and are powered with a GTO (high-voltage gate turnoff thyristors) powering four asynchronous motors. Like the Boston cars, these have three trucks with one set unpowered. Moveable steps accommodate high-level platforms in the Muni Metro subway and street access on surface lines.

Los Angeles bought a fleet of fifty Breda type 2550 LRVs featuring four trucks in a B-B-2-B wheel arrangement. These have front ends attractively painted gray with elegant white stripes and classic stainless-steel side fluting and are assigned to the LA-Pasadena Gold Line.

ABOVE: Cleveland's Regional Transit Authority bought forty-eight Breda LRVs in the early 1980s to replace a worn out fleet of PCC cars. *Walter E. Zullig*

OPPOSITE: A pair of San Francisco Muni Breda-built LRVs descend the grade through Dolores Park on the J-Church Line. *Brian Solomon*

KINKISHARYO
LIGHT RAIL CARS

Kinkisharyo is a subsidiary of Kinki Nippon Railways, one of Japan's oldest and most extensive privately owned networks. The railway has its origins in the old Osaka Electric Tramway, built to connect Osaka and the historic Japanese capital at Nara. The railcar manufacturing subsidiary was founded in 1920, changing its name to Kinki Sharyo in 1945. The firm and its subsidiaries have undergone several name adjustments over the years. (It has been building light rail cars for American urban transit systems since 1986 but will be referred to as Kinkisharyo for simplicity.) Various styles and configurations of its cars can be found on six light rail systems in the United States, making the company among the more prolific suppliers of light rail cars in North America. These cars exhibit distinct body styles and do not have a family resemblance, despite being built by the same manufacturer. Design specifics vary from city to city, with fundamental component such as the

An outbound Kinkisharyo Type 7s and Breda Type 8s, which often work in mixed pairs, approaches Coolidge Corner in Boston, May 2015. *Brian Solomon*

propulsion and articulation systems varying among cars ordered by different city systems. All cars use an articulated design, with most being of the common six-axle three-section type.

Boston's MBTA Green Line was Kinkisharyo's first North American light rail customer, acquiring one hundred cars in 1986 (3600 to 3699), followed by another twenty (3700 to 3719) in 1997. (MBTA's internal classification for these cars is Type 7.) Since then, Kinkisharyo cars have been acquired by: Dallas Area Rapid Transit (DART); NJ Transit's Newark Light Rail and Hudson-Bergen Light Rail systems; Santa Clara, California's Valley Transportation Authority (VTA); Phoenix, Arizona's Valley Metro Light Rail; and most recently Seattle, Washington's SoundTransit Link light rail. Boston's cars are the shortest and lightest, measuring 74 feet over coupler faces and weigh 85,000 pounds when empty. The DART cars are the longest and heaviest, with extended eight-axle cars measuring 123.5 feet, weighing 140,000 pounds empty. Boston's cars use a Westinghouse propulsion system with double-reduction gearing.

Santa Clara, California's Valley Transportation Authority's Kinkisharyo cars are among the most unusual-looking light rail cars operating in America today.
Brian Solomon

BOMBARDIER
FLEXITY TRAMS

Bombardier is major supplier in the world light rail vehicle/ tram market. Yet, while its Flexity trams are widely used across Europe, as of 2015 they have only a small foothold in North America. The Flexity family of similar LRVs is built on a modular concept that is equivalent to that of Bombardier's TRAXX family of locomotives. Bombardier was a pioneer in low-floor light rail design, and today most of its LRVs feature low-floor designs, with several types offering 100 percent low floor. In addition to building LRVs, Bombardier designs and builds entire light rail networks.

The Flexity family covers several different types of LRVs. A variation of the Flexity Outlook has been ordered for service in Toronto, Ontario, and are being constructed domestically at Thunder Bay, Ontario. The prototypes were delivered in 2012, and ultimately the fleet will be used to replace the 1980s-era CLRVs that have dominated Toronto Transit Commission's streetcar lines for more than thirty years.

Flexity Swift is one of the most common and widely accepted Bombardier type, featuring all-powered axles for rapid acceleration. This is one of two types of light rail vehicles operated in the Twin Cities of Minneapolis–St. Paul, Minnesota, by regional transit operator Metro Transit. The first type of modern car used by Metro Transit upon reintroduction of light rail in June 2004, they are primarily assigned to the Blue Line, a north-south route originally called the Hiawatha Line. These twenty-four cars are numbered 101 to 124. They use a 70 percent low-floor design and measure 94 feet long and just over 8 feet 8 inches wide. Top speed is 55 miles per hour and stated passenger capacity is 66 seated and 180 standing.

Bombardier intend to expand its share of the North American light rail vehicle market with a concept tram—a variation of its successful cars—called the Flexity Freedom, to be built in North America. This is available as a 100 percent low-floor car with a step-less interior space. The cars can be built 8 feet 8.5 inches wide with standard two by two seating and wide aisles. Variations are offered with three and five sections and may be built as either a single-end or double-end arrangement; they can be built with multiple-unit capability allowing for trains of up to four cars.

Minneapolis–St. Paul's Metro Transit often decorates its cars with paid advertising. This Bombardier Flexity Swift car promotes a popular brand of beer as it glides though downtown Minneapolis. With the opening of its east-west Green Line in 2014, Metro Transit introduced a fleet of fifty-nine Siemens cars. These share a similar appearance Metro-Transit's Flexity Swifts. *Brian Solomon*

Rapid Transit

MBTA RAPID TRANSIT

In addition to its Green Line light rail and streetcar routes, Boston-centered Massachusetts Bay Transportation Authority operates three entirely separate, heavy electrified, rapid transit routes. Each has its own fleet of cars custom built to fit individual clearance requirements. MBTA color-coded its rapid transit lines in 1965, and although there have been changes to routes over the last fifty years, the color-coding remains key to route identity. Its Blue Line runs from a downtown turning loop at Bowdoin to Wonderland, using a portion of an old trolley subway and the former right-of-way of one-time narrow-gauge electrified Boston, Revere Beach & Lynn. In the subway, cars draw current from line-side third rail, while on the surface they take power from overhead electrification. The transition between electrification is made at the airport station.

Between 2007 and 2009, Siemens supplied ninety-four cars, designated by MBTA as Blue Line Type 4, which replaced 1970s-era Type 3 cars built by Hawker-Siddeley. At

OPPOSITE: Miami-Dade Transit Metro uses Budd-built rapid transit cars. *Walter E. Zullig*

BELOW: In May 2015, a set of out-of-service Bombardier-built cars glides through the Ashmont Station on Boston's MBTA Red Line. *Brian Solomon*

Since the early 1980s, Boston's MBTA Orange Line operations have used a fleet of 120 uniform Hawker-Siddeley cars. *Tim Doherty*

48 feet 6 inches long, these are the shortest cars used by any of the three rapid transit lines. The Orange Line runs on a north-south alignment from Oakgrove to Forest Hill. In downtown Boston, the route is in a subway and is largely on the surface at either end, using alignments built in the 1970s and 1980s to replace the route's traditional elevated railway structure.

As of 2015, the Orange Line was operated using 120 Hawker-Siddeley cars dating from 1981; the cars are 65 feet long but otherwise similar to the former Blue line Type 3s. New cars are on order with the first expected in 2018.

The Red Line has a two-prong route running from Alewife (north of Boston) to branches respectively serving Ashmont and South Braintree. With 218 cars, Red Line has the largest fleet and the longest cars (69 feet 6 inches). The oldest cars were the Red Line Type 1s built by Pullman-Standard during 1969 and 1970. These were augmented in the late 1980s by the Red Line Type 2 cars, which have similar specifications but were built by UTDC. The Red Line Type 3 are the newest cars, built by Bombardier during 1993 and 1994. New Red Line cars are on order.

NEW YORK CITY
RAPID TRANSIT

New York City's urban rail transit is the eight-hundred-pound gorilla of North American transit systems. The largest element of this system is New York's Metropolitan Transportation Authority Subway rapid-transit network (run by the New York City Transit Authority—NYCTA) centered on Manhattan, with routes radiating to Brooklyn, Queens, and the Bronx. In 2014, this consisted of twenty-four lines, covering 659 track miles carrying just under 7.7 million daily passengers. Historically, this was comprised of three systems operated by the Interborough Rapid Transit (IRT), Brooklyn-Manhattan Transit (BMT), and the Independent Subway (IND). The system is a mix of underground subway lines, ground-level running (some of which has been converted from conventional railroad routes), and elevated lines running on steel or concrete structures above city streets. Today, the IRT is system A, while the BMT-IND network is system B, each of which uses separated fleets

System A's class R-188 cars have a retro appearance, despite their relatively modern design. These were built by Kawasaki in 2012. A set of R-188s rattles along the former IRT Flushing Line in Queens. *Jack May*

New York City's oldest rapid transit cars are the Budd-built class R-32/R-32A from 1963. Vintage sets of Budd cars meet at Marcy Avenue in Brooklyn in June 2015. *Brian Solomon*

of rapid-transit cars owing to historic differences in loading gauge. System A routes use numbered identification, while System B routes are lettered. A combined fleet of 6,366 transit cars work these lines. System A cars are 51 feet 0.5 inches long and 8 feet 10.5 inches wide; System B cars are 60 feet 2.5 inches long, and 9 feet 9.3 inches wide.

Historically, cars were manufactured by American railcar producers including Pullman-Standard, St. Louis Car, American Car & Foundry, and the Budd Company. Modern cars have been built by international railcar suppliers, including Alstom, Bombardier, and Kawasaki. The oldest cars in the fleet are R-32/R-32A cars built by Budd in 1964. Of the 600 R-32 cars assigned to System B, as of 2014 only 222 were reported remaining in service. Examples of System A cars include R-62s built by Kawasaki between 1984-1986, and similar R-62As built by Bombardier in the 1980s. For detailed rosters and car descriptions, visit www.nycsubway.org.

Today, New York subway cars can be characterized by clean stainless-steel exteriors and functional interiors. This is a sharp contrast to the mid-1970s, when the rapid-transit system attracted world-wide attention for its cars that were completely covered by graffiti. Interestingly, although graffiti has been largely eradicated from the New York Subway, the spray-paint style of graffiti art made famous in New York has been emulated around the world, and today continues to cover much of the North American freight car fleet.

NYCTA also operates the isolated Staten Island Rapid Transit on its namesake island. Service utilizes sixty-three cars that share specifications with System B cars.

MIAMI-DADE TRANSIT
METRO RAIL

Miami-Dade Transit operates a largely elevated metro-style urban transit system centered on Miami, Florida. Operation began in 1984 and the core system was completed in phases by 1986. Extensions were opened in 2003 and 2012, and by 2015, the operation consisted of a 25-mile, 23-station system with one primary route operated as its Green Line (Palmetto-Dadeland South) and a branch service to the Miami International Airport operated as its Orange Line (Miami International Airport to Earlington Heights over the same tracks to Dadeland South).

The original fleet of cars was ordered from the Budd Company as part of a joint order with Baltimore's Metro-Subway. This was one of Budd's final productions and consisted of 136 cars for Miami built between 1983 and 1984. The cars are 75 feet 1.5 inches long and 10 feet 2 inches wide. They are typically operated in four-car sets, although stations are designed for six cars that could accommodate up to one thousand passengers at a time when fully loaded. A new fleet of cars is on order from AnsaldoBreda expected to be entirely delivered and operational in 2018.

Since it initiated service in 1984, the Miami-Dade Transit Metro has operated with a fleet of Budd-built cars. These are technically similar to cars on Baltimore's rarely photographed rapid transit system. *Walter E. Zullig*

MONTREAL METRO

One of the more unusual rapid-transit systems in North America is the Montreal Metro. This consists of four color-coded routes (Blue, Green, Orange, and Yellow), which crisscross the historic city. The blue line opened first with service beginning in mid-October 1966. Today, the system extends over 43 miles with sixty-eight stations. Montreal Metro's distinctive feature is that its cars ride on rubber tires, and while several French metro systems use a similar arrangement, and cities around the world have adopted rubber tire metros, Montreal's was the world's first entirely rubber-tired metro.

Montreal faces extraordinarily harsh winter conditions, which have led to extensive underground urban development; keeping the entire metro system below ground avoided the obvious problems that arise when rubber tires encounter ice and snow. The advantages of rubber tire operation are superior adhesion, allowing the trains to rapidly ascend relatively steep gradients, and much quieter operation. Visitors to Montreal will be quick to note the muted sounds of the trains. The original fleet of cars, class MR-63, was built by Canadian Vickers, and were augmented in the 1970s by class MR-73s. The latest fleet, class MPM-10, built by Alstom-Bombardier, began arriving in 2014.

Montreal Metro's class MR-73 cars were built by Bombardier in 1976. The 79-series are motor cars, while the 78-series are trailers. Montreal uses a rubber-tire system—notice the unorthodox arrangement of wheels oriented at right angles to each other. *Tim Doherty*

TORONTO TRANSIT COMMISSION
RAPID-TRANSIT CARS

TTC operates four rapid-transit routes in addition to an extensive light rail system. Line 1, which opened in 1954 and is now called the Yonge-University Line, features a U-shaped route serving thirty-two stations. Line 2 is the Bloor-Danforth route with thirty-one stations. Most unusual is the Scarborough Line (Line 3)—a six-station shuttle-extension at the east end of the Bloor-Danforth route that opened in 1984, using a custom-designed fleet of model ICTS cars from former car builder UTDC, powered by a modern linear induction system. The newest route is east-west line 4, called the Sheppard Subway.

TTC's T-1 cars (5000 to 5371) were built by Bombardier in the mid-1990s, soon after it acquired UTDC. The cars are approximately 74 feet 5.5 inches long, and 10 feet 3.5 inches wide. Maximum design speed is 55 miles per hour, while top service speed is 50 miles per hour. They entered service beginning in 1996 and replaced older H-1 and H-2 cars. TTC's most modern cars are the TR class "Toronto Rocket" cars (5381 to 6176), operated in semi-permanent six-car articulated sets that measure slightly less than 460 feet long. Bombardier built 234 units that began entering service in 2011.

Toronto's stylish "Toronto Rocket" cars were built by Bombardier and operate semi-permanently coupled six-car articulated train-sets. These entered traffic in 2011. *Jack May*

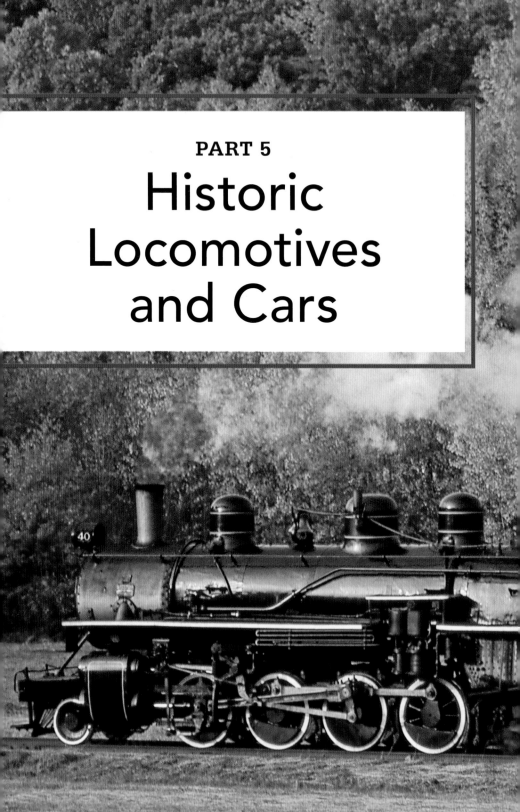

PART 5
Historic Locomotives and Cars

INTRODUCTION

Across North America and around the world, thousands of pieces of historic railway equipment have been set aside for preservation, many restored to their original appearance and kept in operating condition.

The steam locomotive reigned supreme from the dawn of the railway age in the 1820s until it was gradually phased out in favor of diesel-electric power during the 1940s and 1950s. When steam was finally vanquished from the rails depended on the individual railroad. New York, Susquehanna & Western was effectively dieselized by the end of World War II, while most railroads completed dieselization in stages, with the last steam runs being made in the mid-1950s. A handful of large railroads held out longer, notably Canadian Pacific, Duluth, Missabe & Iron Range, and Norfolk

& Western, which kept big steam on the mainline until 1960. Afterwards, pockets of steam survived for a few more years on a few secondary lines. Rio Grande continued to use steam in revenue freight service on its narrow-gauge lines until the end of narrow-gauge common carrier operations in the late 1960s.

Overseas, railways were slower to phase out steam operations. The Republic of Ireland was the first significant country in Europe to end steam operations, when the fires were dumped in 1963. Interestingly, Ireland was also the first country in Western Europe to make widespread use of imported EMD diesels from the United States. Britain, which had originated the concept of the steam railway and exported it around the world, continued to build new

Norfolk & Western J class 4-8-4 611 was restored to service in the spring of 2015. *Brian Solomon*

PREVIOUS PAGE: Valley Railroad No. 40 is an Alco-built 2-8-2 Mikado. *Brian Solomon*

In 2015, Reading & Northern gave its Pacific-type number 425 a fresh coat of blue Imron paint.
Patrick Yough

steam locomotives until 1960. Its Class 9F 2-10-0 *Evening Star* was the last new steam engine built for mainline service, but it had a short life and by 1968 steam had finished in the UK.

However, the rapid conversion to diesel and electric power in the UK, combined with an enforced scaling back of the nationalized railway network, set the stage for an intensive railway preservation movement. In the 1960s and 1970s, dozens of preserved railways emerged and hundreds of steam locomotives (and later historic diesel types) were preserved. In addition to privately run historic and tourist railways, steam has continued to make regular appearances on mainline

excursions. The National Railway Museum at York has one of the world's most impressive displays of preserved railway equipment. In Germany, where steam survived into the 1970s, a great many steam locomotives are preserved in working order, and in addition to excursions and museum work, there are regularly scheduled "Plandampfs"—planned steam—where historic locomotives and trains are used to provide normally scheduled services.

In North America, railway preservation has taken less organized and more grassroots approach. Some lines, notably the Baltimore & Ohio and Pennsylvania Railroad, had an early interest in their own history and began setting aside equipment

Norfolk & Western 611 arrives at Manassas, Virginia, on the morning of June 6, 2015. *Brian Solomon*

by the 1890s for preservation and display. However, many railroads made little effort to set aside equipment, leaving it up to third parties to secure equipment for preservation. Some lines, such as New Haven Railroad and the Erie, sent all of their steam to scrap without a thought of preserving their heritage, but most western railroads took a more generous view. The Burlington, Santa Fe, Southern Pacific, and Union Pacific donated many locomotives to communities along their lines and made locomotives available for preservation. Union Pacific went a step further and retained several locomotives for its Heritage Fleet, including its last new passenger steam locomotive, Alco-built 4-8-4 number 844, which was never retired and has continued to work the railroad's excursion trains (and on rare occasions in revenue freight service) to the present day. Despite various official railroad policies and sometime hostile attitudes toward historic preservation, hundreds of North American locomotives were preserved, and dozens of railway museums around the country were established. In addition, tourist railways aimed providing an historic railway experience have helped keep vintage locomotives running and in the public eye.

Among preserved engines that are truly antique locomotives dating back to railroading formative days are machines such as the British-built John Bull, displayed at the Smithsonian in Washington DC; and a Baltimore & Ohio, grasshopper-type steam locomotive, displayed at the B&O Museum in Baltimore, Maryland. While there are examples of preserved equipment from all eras, most historic railway equipment in North America dates from the twentieth century.

The electric streetcar was once a fixture in most American cities. However, the rapid rise of the automotive industry after World War I doomed most streetcar companies. By World War II, the once-common streetcar was disappearing rapidly, while remaining operations made the transition from private to public ownership. Some of the earliest private railway preservation efforts were in New England, where in the 1940s three individual groups took the initiative to preserve street railway and interurban electric cars that were rapidly disappearing. Elsewhere, other electric railway museums were formed to save streetcars and related equipment while providing visitors the opportunity to step back in time and take a spin on restored rolling antiques. In more recent times, several cities that retained streetcar and light rail transit have restored vintage cars for regular operations or acquired authentic replicas for historic service. In addition, the attraction to historic trolleys has resulted in forward-thinking towns and cities installing heritage routes using vintage cars. In 2015, Boston, Philadelphia, San Diego, and San Francisco operated historic PCC cars in regular daily service. New Orleans has a fleet of Perley Thomas cars.

To the true-blue steam enthusiast, the diesel-electric was the demon that doomed steam, an infernal machine without soul or personality. Yet, classic diesels have become one of the largest and most popular areas of preservation. Hundreds of vintage diesels can be found across the continent. These range from unique, historically significant machines such as Central Railroad of New Jersey 1000, recognized as the first commercially successful diesel-electric, to once-common models such as the mass-produced EMD E and F units built in the 1940s and 1950s. More modern locomotives have been preserved as well, with examples of 1970s and 1980s-era General Electric models now working in tourist service.

In addition to locomotives in museums and working in tourist train service, there are a significant number of heritage locomotive retained by the railroad companies. Most of the Class-1 freight carriers have executive business trains hauled by American classics. Some short lines have preferred to operate their daily freights using vintage locomotives, often old Alco or EMD diesels, much to the delight of railway enthusiasts. Genesee Valley Transportation, which operates several short lines in New York and Pennsylvania, maintains a significant fleet of Alco/Montreal Locomotive Works road switchers, which routinely work its lines in revenue service. A number of short lines have continued to employ classic F-units,

despite these locomotive's advanced age and obsolescence.

In general, American railway preservation has secured a more complete representation of diesels than steam power, but there are some significant and interesting diesel models that have been lost. Baldwin, which had been the most prolific steam builder, didn't fare well in its transition as a diesel producer. The company exited the locomotive business in 1956 due to dismal sales. Many of its road locomotives were poorly regarded and barely outlasted the steam locomotives they were bought to replace. Except for switcher models, relatively few Baldwin road models were preserved and virtually nothing is left of its passenger line. Likewise, Fairbanks-Morse, a diesel-engine manufacturer that entered the postwar locomotive market, is poorly represented.

Despite these shortfalls, visitors to railway museums may be surprised to find what has survived the scrapper's torch. In addition to diesel, several types of vintage electric locomotives are prominently represented at railroad museums. More than a dozen examples of Pennsylvania Railroad's famed GG1 survive around the country, with two displayed at the Railroad Museum of Pennsylvania in Strasburg, which also displays a variety of PRR's more curious electrics and the bulk of its preserved steam power, among other historic rolling stock.

Locomotives are often the main focus of railway preservation efforts, yet historic passenger and freight cars have also been preserved in large numbers.

Among the historic equipment represented in these pages is just a small selection of noteworthy and interesting locomotives and streetcars. It cannot possibly do justice to the wide variety of classic equipment preserved or at work in North America and around the world, for which even a basic complete listing could fill volumes.

Historic Steam Locomotives

Replica 4-4-0s, representing Central Pacific's *Jupiter* and Union Pacific No. 119, are posed at Promontory, Utah, marking the historic location where the lines comprising first Transcontinental Railroad were linked in 1869. *Jack May*

PREVIOUS PAGE: Norfolk & Western 611 at Manassas, Virginia. *Brian Solomon*

THE AMERICAN STANDARD 4-4-0

The classic 4-4-0 American Standard, or American type, is the defining nineteenth century North American locomotive, and remains the most familiar engine of all time. By one estimate, more than 25,000 4-4-0s were built for American railroads. Key to its success was the pivoting leading truck that provided the locomotive with a three-point suspension system, giving it flexibility to work on lightly constructed track while still being sufficiently powerful to handle most work.

The 4-4-0 emerged as a universal standard type in the 1840s and 1850s when the American railway network was growing rapidly, and it remained dominant until the 1880s.

Among the famous 4-4-0s is Western & Atlantic's *General*, the Civil War-era locomotive commandeered by Union raiders and pursued by Confederate troops. On May 10, 1869, Central Pacific's 4-4-0 *Jupiter* and Union Pacific 4-4-0 No. 119 posed pilot-to-pilot at Promontory, Utah, to mark completion of the first Transcontinental Railroad. Today, operating replicas of these famous engines make regular re-enactments of the event at the site.

PENNSYLVANIA RAILROAD 1223 SPECIFICATIONS (DISPLAYED AT THE RAILROAD MUSEUM OF PENNSYLVANIA)

Type: PRR Class D-16sb, light passenger engine

Manufacturer: PRR's Juniata Shops

Year Built: 1905

Wheel Arrangement: 4-4-0

Driving Wheels: 68 in.

Engine Weight: 141,000 lbs.

Cylinders: 20.5 x 26 in.

Tractive Effort: 23,900 lbs.

THE 0-6-0 STEAM SWITCHER

Engines with the 0-6-0 wheel arrangement that originated in England were among the earliest types of steam locomotives. Originally a heavy road freight engine, the lack of leading wheels made it impractical for road service in the United States, where operation on lightly built track required a more flexible and more advanced locomotive type with guiding wheels. After the American Civil War, the 0-6-0 evolved as switcher. Here, simple construction made the type inexpensive, and because all wheels were powered, they had comparatively high tractive effort for their size. The 0-6-0 switchers were built in large numbers into the twentieth century. Typically, they were tasked with slow-speed work where their short wheelbase allowed them to negotiate sharp curves and serve sidings and spurs where road locomotives were ill-suited or prohibited because of their size and weight. By one estimate, some fifteen thousand 0-6-0s were built for domestic use, making it one of the most numerous types in North America. This includes locomotives built by major manufacturers such as Baldwin, as well smaller builders, such as Porter and Vulcan, which constructed stock locomotives for industrial applications. Many 0-6-0s were built as self-contained tank engines (without a tender). More than 110 were preserved and they are commonly found at railroad museums and working tourist trains.

BALDWIN NUMBER 26 SPECIFICATIONS, DISPLAYED AT STEAMTOWN IN SCRANTON

Type: Medium-size switcher

Manufacturer: Baldwin Locomotive Works

Year Built: 1929

Wheel Arrangement: 0-6-0

Driving Wheels: 50 in.

Engine Weight: 124,000 lbs.

Cylinders: 20 x 24 in.

Tractive Effort: 29,375 lbs.

Max. Operating Speed: NA

A common variation of the 0-6-0 was a tank engine 0-6-0T that carried its own fuel and water without a separate tender. This Porter-built engine is preserved at Strasburg, Pennsylvania. *Richard Jay Solomon*

SHAY GEARED LOCOMOTIVES

Industrial railroads, such as logging lines where poor track, steep grades and slow speeds were common, required specialized steam locomotives that could provide high tractive power while maintaining high adhesion at slow speeds on rough track. So instead of conventional reciprocating engines typical of mainline operations (with direct connections between piston and drivers), geared locomotives were developed with cylinders that powered wheels indirectly: Cylinders turned a crankshaft using reduction gearing to power swiveling trucks. This provided good wheel-to-rail contact while allowing for continuous slow-speed working necessary to negotiate very steep grades.

The first and most common geared engine was the Shay type built by the Lima Locomotive Works of Lima, Ohio. This type used a row of vertical cylinders on the engineer's side of the engine to turn a longitudinal crankshaft, similar in concept to that used in automobiles, which powered pivoting trucks at the ends of the locomotive. Both two-truck and three-truck Shays were built. The final locomotive was built in 1945 as Western Maryland No. 6, a three-truck type that was also the largest Shay ever built. Several tourist railroads specialized in Shay operations, including the Roaring Camp and Big Trees in California, and West Virginia's Cass Scenic Railroad.

WESTERN MARYLAND NUMBER 6 SPECIFICATIONS

Type: Three-Truck Shay

Year Built: 1945

Manufacturer: Lima Locomotive Works

Wheel Arrangement: B-B-B (or 040-040-040T)

Railroad: Western Maryland

Driving Wheels: 48 in.

Engine Weight: 324,000 lbs.

Cylinders: Three 17 x 18 in.

Tractive Effort: 59,700 lbs.

Max. Operating Speed: NA

Gauge: 4 ft. 8.5 in.

Narrow-gauge Shay Dixiana is one of several geared steam locomotives preserved in working order on the Roaring Camp & Big Trees Railroad at Fulton, California. This 42-ton engine was built by Lima in 1912 and has been designated a National Mechanical Engineering Historic Landmark. *Brian Solomon*

CLIMAX AND HEISLER GEARED LOCOMOTIVES

Less-common geared locomotives than the Shay-type manufactured by Lima, were similar engines built in Pennsylvania by the Climax Manufacturing Company of Corry, and the Heisler Locomotive Works in Erie. The Climax type used a pair of steeply angled cylinders on opposite sides of the boiler, oriented parallel to it, to drive the crankshaft. The Heisler featured a pair of steeply angled cylinders arranged cross-wise below the boiler and oriented at a 90-degree angle to each other. Like the Shay, Heislers could be ordered in either two-truck or three-truck arrangements.

Geared locomotives were common on lumber railways, and were operated on lightly built lines in northern New England, the Appalachians, upper Midwest, northern California, and the Pacific Northwest. On a few lines, the agile abilities of these steam engines allowed them to work into the 1960s, years after most mainline steam had been retired. Both types can be found operating on American tourist railways where their slow speed operation is well suited to the relaxed pace offered by tourist trains.

Freeport, Illinois-based Silver Creek & Stephenson operates this 1912-built Heisler, which has worked for various lumber company lines in Mississippi and South Carolina before being adopted as a tourist train locomotive. *Dan Howard*

2-8-2 MIKADO

The 2-8-2 Mikado-type locomotive was one of the most widely built American locomotive types of the twentieth century, with an estimated ten thousand built for domestic service and more than four thousand for export. The type was first developed for export in the late nineteenth century, and famously got its unusual name as a result of Baldwin Locomotive Works order for the type from Japanese Railways at a time when the comic opera *The Mikado*, about Japan's emperor, was enjoying American popularity. However, during World War II, some American nationalists attempted to change the name to the *MacArthur-type* after the popular American general.

Northern Pacific was the first large railroad to adopt the Mikado on large scale, and by World War I, it had become a dominant type for general freight service, owing to its large firebox and good traction qualities without excessive axle loading.

A large number of Mikados have been preserved. Interestingly, while the type was rarely used as a passenger locomotive in the steam era, it has become one of the more common varieties on American tourist roads. In addition to historic locomotives, several modern Chinese-built 2-8-2s have been imported for tourist operations in the United States.

MIKADO EXAMPLE SPECIFICATIONS

Type: Pennsylvania Railroad Class L1s (superheated)

Manufacturers: PRR's Juniata Shops, Baldwin

Years Built: 1914-1919

Number Built: 574

Wheel Arrangement: 2-8-2 Mikado

Railroad: Pennsylvania Railroad

Driving Wheels: 62 in.

Engine Weight: 320,700 lbs.

Cylinders: 27 x 30 in.

Tractive Effort: 61,465 lbs.

The Texas State Railroad restored former Magma Arizona 2-8-2 Mikado number 7 to service in 2014. Today it is a popular excursion engine as pictured at Palestine, Texas. *Tom Kline*

Cumbres & Toltec Scenic K36 number 484 drifts at Windy Point. *Brian Solomon*

NARROW GAUGE MIKADOS

Narrow Gauge 2-8-2 Mikados have enjoyed a high profile presence on popular American tourist lines, notably the former Rio Grande engines on the Durango & Silverton and Cumbres & Toltec Scenic Railroads in Colorado and New Mexico, and on Pennsylvania's unique East Broad Top line.

In 1903, Baldwin built fifteen unusual 2-8-2s with outside frames and counterweights (to compensate for space restrictions between the wheels) for Rio Grande. These were class K27s, and colloquially known as *Mud hens* for their squat appearance with small drivers and a relatively big boiler, and their ability to stir up the ballast. In 1923, Rio Grande bought ten more three-foot gauge 2-8-2s—these were class K28 and built by Alco. A couple of years later, Baldwin built their class K36s. Finally, in 1928 and 1930, the Rio Grande's Burnham Shops (Denver) converted ten standard-gauge 2-8-0 Consolidations into heavy narrow-gauge 2-8-2s, class K37.

Between 1911 and 1920, Baldwin built six more conventional designed three-foot gauge 2-8-2s for Pennsylvania coal-line East Broad Top. All survived when the railroad ended common carrier operations in 1956, and four were later revived for tourist train service. As of 2015, EBT was dormant and its 2-8-2s are stored at its roundhouse in Rock Hill Furnace, Pennsylvania.

DENVER & RIO GRANDE CLASS K-36 SPECIFICATIONS

Type: Narrow gauge Mikado

Manufacturer: Baldwin

Years Built: 1925

Number Built: 10

Road Numbers: 480 to 489

Wheel Arrangement: 2-8-2 Mikado

Drivers: 44 in.

Engine Weight: 187,000 lbs.

Cylinders: 20 x 24 in.

Tractive Effort: 36,200 lbs.

Max. Operating Speed: NA

Gauge: 3 ft.

PACIFICS

The 4-6-2 Pacific-type wheel arrangement offered a logical expansion of the 4-4-2 Atlantic and common 4-6-0 types, and it rapidly gained favor in the early years of the twentieth century as a heavy passenger locomotive. It was widely built for North American lines from 1903 until after World War II, and until replaced by diesels in the 1950s, it epitomized American twentieth century passenger power. To a lesser extent, the type was also developed as a fast-road freight locomotive.

Many Pacifics were preserved and a few have had high-profile careers as modern-day excursion engines, including several engines built for Canadian Pacific. Southern Pacific P-8 Pacific 2472 built by Baldwin was restored to service in 1991 and has worked trips on home rails in California. In Pennsylvania, former Gulf, Mobile & Northern 425 has worked for three decades on Reading & Northern lines. Unquestionably, the most famous Pacific type is the Pennsylvania Railroad K4s ("s" for superheat, not for plural). Two were preserved: Engine 1361 displayed for years at the Horseshoe Curve near Altoona and was briefly restored to service in the late 1980s, while hopes for its second restoration have been beset with difficulties; 3750 is a static display at the Railroad Museum of Pennsylvania at Strasburg.

PENNSYLVANIA RAILROAD K4S PACIFIC SPECIFICATIONS

Type: K4s for express passenger service

Manufacturer: Baldwin, PRR Juniata Shops

Years Built: 1914-1928

Number Built: 425

Wheel Arrangement: 4-6-2

Driving Wheels: 80 in.

Engine Weight: 310,500 lbs.

Cylinders: 27 x 28 in.

Tractive Effort: 44,400 lbs.

Reading & Northern's 4-6-2 Pacific number 425 was built by the Baldwin Locomotive Works in January 1928 for Gulf, Mobile & Northern (a component company of the Gulf, Mobile & Ohio system). *Brian Solomon*

New York, Chicago & St. Louis No. 765 is a Lima 2-8-4 Berkshire built in 1944, and one of several surviving examples of the type. It is operated by the Ft. Wayne Railroad Historical Society. *Patrick Yough*

NICKEL PLATE ROAD BERKSHIRE

In the mid-1920s, Lima expanded the 2-8-2 Mikado into the 2-8-4 Berkshire type for the New York Central System's Boston & Albany. The type was named for B&A's Berkshire crossing. Lima engineered a larger firebox and boiler to supply ample amounts of steam for comparatively fast freight service in heavily graded territory. This required the first application of the radial load-bearing four-wheel trailing truck. Early 2-8-4s had 63-inch drivers, ideal for moving freight in graded territory but not as practical for fast work on level track.

The Berkshire's later evolution was due to the Van Sweringen brothers of Cleveland, Ohio. Their new railroad empire of the 1920s and 1930s included the Chesapeake & Ohio, Erie, and Nickel Plate Road, which connected Buffalo with Chicago and St. Louis). Van Sweringen's operating genius, John J. Bernet, saw the 2-8-4's potential and ordered a fleet of Alco-2-8-4s for the Erie in which the design was pushed forward by using precision-balanced

NICKEL PLATE ROAD CLASS S-2 SPECIFICATIONS

Type: Road freight engine

Manufacturer: Lima

Years Built: 1944

Number Built: 10

Wheel Arrangement: 2-8-4 Berkshire

Driving Wheels: 69 in.

Engine Weight: 440,800 lbs.

Cylinders: 25 x 34 in.

Tractive Effort: 64,100 lbs.

70-inch drivers. The Van Sweringens created the Advisory Mechanical Committee to establish well-engineered standard designs for the different railroads. In 1933, Bernet focused on Nickel Plate's fleet, and the AMC drafted for the line a top-performing 2-8-4. The first of these machines were built for Nickel Plate by Alco in 1934 (700 to 714). Between 1942 and 1943, Lima built fifty-five more 2-8-4s for the line; and curiously in 1949, Nickel Plate, rather than investing in freight diesels, opted for ten more 2-8-4s. Lima's final order for Berkshires concluded with Nickel Plate Road 779, also the last Lima steam ever built.

Nickel Plate's Berkshires shared common qualities with other AMC-designed modern steam, which were admired for a solid, well-balanced appearance with attributes such as extra-large sand domes featuring multiple external sand-line feeds. Van Sweringen's other lines bought similar 2-8-4s, including Pere Marquette, Wheeling, and C&O (called Kanawas). Nickel Plate worked its 2-8-4s on time freights noted for exceptional speed, and were among the only steam power known to regularly haul "piggy back" trailers. The railroad discontinued mainline steam in 1958.

Several AMC Berkshires have been preserved, and Nickel Plate engines earned national fame for excursion work. Nickel Plate 759 was a high-profile engine in the 1960s and early 1970s and today is a static display at Steamtown in Scranton, Pennsylvania. NKP 765, based in Fort Wayne, Indiana, continues excursion work.

Nickel Plate Road 765 makes an impressive show of smoke leading the Lehigh Gorge Special across the Lehigh River at Weissport, Pennsylvania, on August 23, 2015. *Patrick Yough*

The restored Grand Truck Western class U3b 4-8-4 6325 works an excursion on the Ohio Central in October 2002. GTW was a Canadian National subsidiary in the United States, and its 4-8-4s were similar CNs. *Brian Solomon*

4-8-4 NORTHERNS

Northern Pacific was first to adopt the 4-8-4, working with Alco in 1926 to develop this new wheel arrangement for long-distance passenger service. NP's pioneers arrived in 1927, and soon several other railroads developed 4-8-4s. This wheel arrangement was a natural progression of the 4-8-2 Mountain, 2-8-4 Berkshire, and 4-6-4 Hudson types. It was well suited to freight and passenger service, but while a few lines, such as Santa Fe, bought 4-8-4s for dual traffic, in practice most railroads ordered 4-8-4s for either mainline freight or passenger work.

NP gave the type its common name, *Northern*, but no other steam locomotive wheel arrangement has had more names than the 4-8-4: on the Lackawanna they were *Poconos*, Lehigh Valley called them *Wyomings*, to Canadian National they were *Confederations*, Chesapeake & Ohio's were *Greenbriers*, while New York Central and National Railways of Mexico knew them as *Niagaras*.

The 4-8-4 was the most common of the late-era North American steam locomotive wheel arrangements, and roughly one thousand were built. Canadian National Railway and its American subsidiary Grand Trunk Western had the largest number, 203 locomotives represented by several different classes. But these were atypical because CN's 4-8-4s were designed with comparatively light axle weight to give them great route flexibility and were operated widely on its vast North American network. By contrast, some roads, such as Chicago & North Western, bought 4-8-4s strictly for their heaviest mainlines.

NORFOLK & WESTERN J CLASS SPECIFICATIONS

Type: Express passenger engine

Manufacturer: N&W Roanoke Shops

Years Built: 1941-950

Number Built: 13

Wheel Arrangement: 4-8-4

Driving Wheels: 70 in.

Engine Weight: 494,000 lbs.

Cylinders: 27 x 32 in.

Tractive effort: 80,000 lbs.

Max. Operating Speed: 110 mph (est.)

Southern Pacific GS4 4449 works Brock, California, on April 28, 1991. *Brian Solomon*

On several railroads the 4-8-4 was refined as a thoroughbred—supremely engineered locomotives that have remained among the best-regarded modern steam. Santa Fe's 3765 and 2900 class, Southern Pacific's semi-streamlined Gs4 and Gs5s, Union Pacific's 800 series, and Norfolk & Western's elegant streamlined J-class were among the finest locomotives on American rails.

The 4-8-4 has remained as a popular class for main line excursions and over the last four decades various engines have worked North American mainlines, while many of the type are preserved in museums. Among the best-known 4-8-4s are Reading Company's class T-1s. Santa Fe's pioneer 4-8-4 engine 3751 has worked high-profile trips on the West Coast, as has Spokane, Portland & Seattle engine 700. Milwaukee Road 261 has been a star of Midwestern mainline trips. The three most famous 4-8-4s are Southern Pacific 4449, a streamlined engine, class Gs4, built by Lima in 1941 for work on the *Daylight* trains; Union Pacific 844, the last of the railroad's passenger steam turned out by Alco in 1944 and which has remained on the roster continuously ever since; and Norfolk & Western J-Class 611, which was famously returned to service in 1982, and again in 2015.

CHALLENGER

One of the first, and by far the most successful high-speed articulated steam locomotive, was the 4-6-6-4 Challenger type developed by Union Pacific and Alco in 1936. The 4-6-6-4's four-wheel leading truck and tall driving wheels with a large boiler and well-engineered suspension and innovative articulated connections allowed for smooth running at higher speeds. Unlike earlier simple articulated engines designed to be operated at a maximum of 30 to 35 miles per hour, UP's Challenger was capable of 80 miles per hour. It was a huge, powerful machine and yet by keeping axle-weight within normal limits allowed the type great operational flexibility.

More than 250 Challengers were built in the United States. With 105 of them, UP had the largest fleet, but it wasn't the only railroad to adopt the 4-6-6-4: Clinchfield, Delaware & Hudson, Northern Pacific, Rio Grande, Spokane, Portland & Seattle, and Western Pacific operated Alco-built challengers; Baldwin 4-6-6-4s for Rio Grande, and Western Maryland.

Owing to their late-era development, many Challengers had very short service lives, operating for less than ten years before being sidelined by more efficient diesels. UP preserved two: 3977 is displayed at North Platte, Nebraska; engine 3985 was restored for excursion service in 1981, and presently resides at UP's roundhouse in Cheyenne, Wyoming.

UNION PACIFIC CHALLENGER SPECIFICATIONS

Type: Road freight and passenger engine

Manufacturer: Alco

Years Built: 1936-1943

Wheel Arrangement: 4-6-6-4, Challenger

Driving Wheels: 69 in.

Overall Length: 121 ft. 11 in. (with tender)

Engine Weight: 627,000 lbs.

Cylinders: Four 21 x 32 in.

Tractive effort: 97,350 lbs.

Max. Operating Speed: 80 mph

In 1992, Union Pacific Challenger 3985 worked the former Western Pacific line over Altamont Pass in California. *Brian Solomon*

UNION PACIFIC
BIG BOY

Union Pacific's massive Big Boy is defined by its unique 4-8-8-4 wheel arrangement. It has often been regarded as the largest steam locomotive ever built, and its only contender is the Lima-built 2-6-6-6 Allegheny built for Chesapeake & Ohio and Virginian. The Big Boy was an outgrowth of UP's success with the 4-6-6-4 Challenger, and specifically designed to singly handle heavy freights from Ogden, Utah, to Cheyenne, Wyoming, where the eastbound accent of the Wasatch Mountains just east of Odgen and UP's was the defining grade. UP worked with Alco in designing the 4-8-8-4, and on September 4, 1941, the first of twenty-five Big Boys was delivered to Union Pacific at Council Bluffs, Iowa. Although a freight hauler, Big Boy was designed for both power and speed and could easily reach 70 miles per hour. Big Boys were capable of hauling passenger trains but rarely saw regular passenger duties. Big Boys survived later than most American steam, with some working until 1958 hauling freight over Wyoming's Sherman Hill. Eight of the locomotives were preserved. In 2014, UP made big news when it moved Big Boy 4014 from its long-time static display at Pomona, California, to Cheyenne, Wyoming, in preparation for restoration to service.

UNION PACIFIC BIG BOY SPECIFICATIONS

Type: Heavy road-freight steam locomotive

Manufacturer: Alco

Years Built: 1941-1944

Wheel Arrangement: 4-8-8-4, Big Boy

Driving Wheels: 68 in.

Overall Length: 132 ft., 9.375 in. (with tender)

Engine Weight: 772,000 lbs.

Cylinders: Four 23.75 x 32 in.

Tractive effort: 135,375 lbs.

Max. Operating Speed: 70 mph

On August 20, 1957, Union Pacific Big Boy 4015 shook the ground leading an eastward freight near the Hermosa Tunnel on Wyoming's Sherman Hill, west of Cheyenne.
Jim Shaughnessy

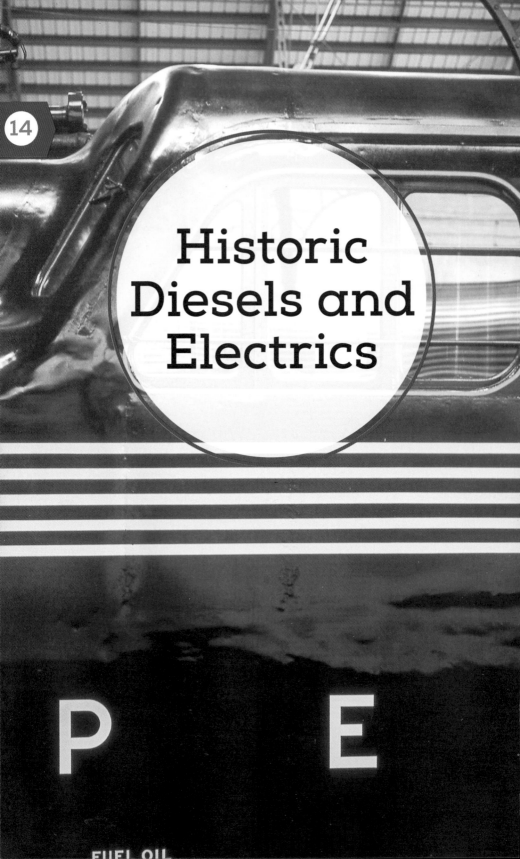

14

Historic Diesels and Electrics

P E

FUEL OIL

Chicago, Milwaukee, St Paul & Pacific "Bi-polar" E-2 is one of several historic electric locomotives displayed at the Museum of Transportation in St. Louis, Missouri. *Brian Solomon*

MILWAUKEE GE BI-POLAR

In 1915, General Electric began wiring Milwaukee Road's recently completed Pacific Extension using its state of the art high-voltage DC system overhead electrification system. By 1927, Milwaukee had two long (but non-contiguous) electrified sections covering more than 660-route mainline miles. Its Cascade electrified section extended over the mountains from Othello, Washington, to Tacoma and Seattle.

For Cascade service, in 1919 GE, working with Alco, constructed five massive three-piece articulated electrics, Milwaukee Road class EP-2. These distinctive machines consisted of a center-cab configuration bracketed with elongated, wagon-top hood end sections using an unusual wheel arrangement, described as 1-B-D+D-B-1. The twelve driving-axles were powered by a General Electric Type 100 gearless bi-polar motor—as a result the EP-2s were known as *Bi-Polars*. They routinely worked transcontinental passenger trains, lifting thousand-ton consists over the 2 percent Cascade grades at 25 miles per hour. The big-electrics were retired in the early 1960s, by which time the railroad had discontinued its transcontinental passenger operations. The Cascade electrification only survived a few more years. Ultimately, Milwaukee entirely abandoned electric operation, ceasing operations to the Pacific altogether in 1980. Milwaukee's lone surviving Bi-Polar is displayed at the Museum of Transportation in St. Louis.

MILWAUKEE BI-POLAR SPECIFICATIONS

Type: Direct current passenger electric

Manufacturer: General Electric-Alco

Years Built: 1918

Wheel Arrangement: 1-B-D+D-B-1

Input Voltage: 3,000 volt DC overhead

Output: 3,200 horsepower

Tractive Effort: 42,000 lbs. at 28.4 mph

Weight: NA

Overall Length: NA

OPPOSITE: PRR GG1 electric 4859 is preserved at Harrisburg, Pennsylvania. *Brian Solomon*

ALCO-GENERAL ELECTRIC-INGERSOLL-RAND
BOX CAB

In the mid-1920s, a consortium between diesel-engine manufacturer Ingersoll-Rand and locomotive builders Alco and GE was formed to construct a prototype box-cab diesel-electric switcher rated at 300 horsepower. Following a demonstration tour in 1924, the consortium built stock locomotives for sale. These diesels had more in common with heavy electrics of the period than with later diesel-electrics developed in the 1930s powered by the next generation of lightweight high-output engines.

Among the applications for diesel switchers were in large cities, especially New York, where early air-quality legislation discouraged the use of steam power, and where the high cost of electrification was not cost effective. Significantly, Central Railroad of New Jersey bought the first of these at the end of 1924 (assigned road number 1000), and this engine is considered to be the first commercially sold diesel-electric locomotive in the United States. CNJ 1000 was assigned to work isolated waterfront trackage in The Bronx, in New York City. From 1925 to 1928, the Alco-GE-IR group built thirty-one box-cab diesel-electrics. Customers included Baltimore & Ohio, Lehigh Valley, and Long Island Rail Road.

CNJ 1000 SPECIFICATIONS

Type: Diesel-electric box-cab switcher

Manufacturer: Assembled by Alco

Year Built: 1925

Wheel Arrangement: B-B

Engine: Ingersoll-Rand 6-cylinder engine

Output: 300 horsepower

Starting Tractive Effort: 30,000 lbs.

Weight: 120,000 lbs.

Overall Length: 32 ft. 8 in.

After more than 30 years of service in The Bronx, New York, Central Railroad of New Jersey 1000 was preserved at the Baltimore & Ohio Museum in Baltimore, Maryland. *Brian Solomon*

PENNSYLVANIA RR
GG1

The Pennsylvania Railroad (PRR) GG1 is a classic American locomotive—an elegant double-ended streamlined speedster. It was the standard electric on PRR's electrified lines for decades. The type dates to 1934, when the railroad deemed that its recently built box-cab electrics were inadequate for the fast passenger service they had been intended to work. PRR had borrowed a New Haven EP-3 electric with the 2-C-C-2 wheel arrangement for testing prior to developing a pair of experimental prototypes, each with similar streamlined center-cab designs. Ultimately, the GG1 won out over the lone class R1 prototype with a 2-D-2 arrangement. Industrial designer Raymond Loewy was hired to refine the GG1 locomotive's styling, and over the next nine years the railroad acquired a fleet of 138 GG1s.

Originally, PRR's GG1s primarily worked passenger services, but in later years some were regeared for freight. The GG1s labored long after the Pennsylvania-New York Central merger of 1968. In the Amtrak-era, the GG1s's run was extended from New York Penn Station to New Haven, Connecticut, over the former the New Haven Railroad. In October 1983, the GG1 concluded its service, the last engines working New Jersey Transit suburban trains. More than a dozen GG1s escaped scrapping; today some survive as static displays in museums around the country.

PENNSYLVANIA RR GG1 SPECIFICATIONS

Type: High-speed electric

Manufacturers: Baldwin-Westinghouse, General Electric, PRR Juniata Shops

Years Built: 1934-1943

Wheel Arrangement: 2-C-C-2

Input Voltage: 11,500 Volts at 25Hz alternating current

Output: 4,620 to 4,930 horsepower

Tractive Effort: 70,700 to 75,000 lbs. (varied depending on weight)

Max. Operating Speed: 100 mph/160 kph

Weight: 460,000 lbs. to 477,000 lbs.

Overall Length: 79 ft. 6 in.

Pennsylvania Railroad GG1 4935 is among many excellent displays at the Railroad Museum of Pennsylvania. *Brian Solomon*

ELECTRO-MOTIVE SW1

The SW1 was one of the few models that straddled its builder's name change from General Motors' Electro-Motive Corporation to GM's Electro-Motive Division.

Built from 1939 and 1953, this low-horsepower switcher was one of the builder's more popular types; powered by a 6-cylinder version of the 567 engine, it was ideal for slow speed applications such as switching freight sidings and working coach yards. A few of these antiques can still be found on American short lines and in museums. Some have worked as shop switchers, where they were treated as pet locomotives and maintained to showroom standards.

Electro-Motive's model designation system evolved over the years, with letters used to signify various attributes at different times. In its 1930s system, "SW" indicated "six-hundred horsepower, welded frame," but obviously the SW connotations also signified "Switcher," and many later EMD switcher models retained the SW prefix despite being more powerful. The SW1 is easily distinguished from other EMD switchers by its shorter hood length, lone narrow exhaust stack, the platform behind the cab, plus the boxy sandbox below the radiator at the hood end.

EMD MODEL SW1 SPECIFICATIONS

Type: Diesel-electric switcher

Manufacturer: Electro-Motive Corporation/EMD

Years Built: 1939-1953

Wheel Arrangement: B-B

Engine: EMD 6-567

Output: 600 horsepower

Tractive Effort: 24,000 lbs. at 10 mph

Max. Operating Speed: 50 mph

Weight: 200,000 lbs.

Overall Length: 44 ft. 5 in.

On May 10, 2008, Western Pacific SW1 501 catches the high-Sierra sun at the Western Pacific Railroad Museum in Portola, California. *Brian Solomon*

General Motors Electro-Motive Corporation's pioneer FT number 103 has been preserved. *Brian Solomon*

ELECTRO-MOTIVE FT

Unquestionably one of the most significant locomotives of the twentieth century was General Motors' Electro-Motive Corporation (soon to be renamed Electro-Motive Division) model FT. The prototype, a four-unit set numbered 103, quietly made its debut in November 1939. This was an elegant streamlined engine designed to awe the railroads. It was painted dark green and cream with "GM" on the front and "Electro-Motive" on its sides. It was America's pioneer mass-produced road-freight locomotive and was instrumental in the widespread conversion from steam to diesel-electric power. On the eve of American involvement in World War II, FT 103 made a famous 83,764 mile tour of twenty Class I railroads. As built, most FT's were married pairs of A-B units with a drawbar between units in place of a conventional coupler. The locomotive used mechanical belt-driven auxiliaries and was the first model to ride on recently developed four-wheel Blomberg trucks.

Santa Fe received the first and largest fleet, consisting of 320 units; in total, twenty-three railroads bought the type. Today, a lone A-B FT set survives—the cab unit from the 103 demonstrator set—normally displayed at the Museum of Transportations in St. Louis.

EMD MODEL FT SPECIFICATIONS

Type: Road service diesel electric

Manufacturer: Electro-Motive Corporation /EMD

Dates Built: 1939-1945

Wheel Arrangement: B-B

Engine: EMD 16-567/16-567A

Output: 1,350 horsepower (per unit)

Tractive Effort: 32,500 lbs. (228,000 lbs. for four-unit set)

Max. Operating Speed: 65 mph

Weight: 230,000 lbs. (A-unit)

Overall Length: 48 ft. 3 in. (A-unit)

ALCO RS-1

Alco's RS-1 can be considered the first diesel road switcher, a type that effectively melded switching and road locomotives in one versatile diesel that set the pattern for some of the best-selling locomotives of all time. Alco first sold the type to Rock Island Lines in 1941. At that time, Alco didn't use model designations and the RS-1 designation was retroactively applied but universally accepted. Over the next two decades, more than four hundred RS-1s were built for North American railroads. By 1949, all the major diesel builders were selling road switchers, and during the 1950s the road switcher emerged as the dominant diesel configuration on American railroads.

A variation of the RS-1 was a six-axle RSD-1 a type with world significance, because during World War II Alco built a small fleet for export to the Soviet Union. The USSR copied the type and built thousands of similar diesels based on Alco's RS-1-era technology, and these types remain active in many countries around the world. A few classic Alco RS-1s survive on American short lines, tourist railroads, and museums.

ALCO RS-1 SPECIFICATIONS

Type: Diesel-electric road-switcher

Manufacturer: Alco-GE

Years Built: 1941-1957

Wheel Arrangement: B-B

Engine: Alco 6-539

Output: 1,000 horsepower

Tractive Effort: 34,000 lbs. at 8 mph

Max. Operating Speed: 60 mph with 75:16 gearing

Weight: 238,000 lbs.

Overall Length: 51 ft.

A Chicago & Western Indiana RS-1 works at 16th Street in Chicago, Illinois, in June 1961. *Richard Jay Solomon*

Locomotive 5809 is one of two former Pennsylvania Railroad's E8As privately owned by Juniata Terminal. *Brian Solomon*

E8 AND E9

In 1949, Electro-Motive introduced its E8 model as part of a whole series of new and improved locomotives that replaced older models in its catalog. Significantly, the E8 offered greater power, improved reliability, and simplified maintenance over its predecessor, the E7. Design changes included the used of three-phase AC motor-operated appliances in place of belt-driven exhaust fans and other appliances on the E7. A slightly more powerful version of the 12-567 engine output on the E8 boosted locomotive horsepower to 2,250. The E8 was also Electro-Motive's first A1A-A1A passenger model equipped with dynamic braking. During its five-year production, 421 E8A's were built for American service.

The E9 replaced the E8 in 1955, using a pair of the much-improved 12-567C diesels with combined output of 2,400 horsepower. However, EMD built just one hundred E9As and forty-four E9Bs, owning to a declining market for passenger locomotives. Externally, the E9A exhibited only very minor differences with late-build E8A units. Notably, the headlight housing featured a flush front in contrast with the metal lip on the older headlights.

EMD E9A SPECIFICATIONS

Type: Diesel-electric road passenger

Manufacturer: EMD

Years Built: 1954-1963

Wheel Arrangement: A1A-A1A

Engine: Two EMD 12-567Cs

Output: 2,400 horsepower

Tractive Effort: 19,500 lbs. (continuous with 52:25 gearing)

Max. Operating Speed: 117 mph with 52:25 gearing

Weight: 316,500 lbs.

Overall Length: 70 ft. 3 in.

ELECTRO-MOTIVE DIVISION
MODELS F3, F7, AND F9

Electro-Motive's F-unit models were a dominant locomotive type built in the 1950s. The F units were built in such large numbers that they exceeded the combined total production of all competing builders' diesel-electric units sold in North America at that time. These carbody types featured EMD's characteristic "bulldog" nose. They rode on pairs of twin-axle Blomberg trucks, and were the standard road-service diesels on most railroads across the continent. The F-models, along with EMD's other types, largely supplanted steam on American mainlines.

The F3 was EMD's post-war model successor to the FT, part of a design evolution that had begun with EMD's gas-electric cars of the 1920s. In 1949, EMD introduced its model F7 to supersede the F3. Both models were rated at 1,500 horsepower, but the F7 embodied a variety of technological refinements intended to lower maintenance costs and increase tractive effort. These models suited the needs of American railways during the fever of postwar dieselization. An estimated 2,366 F7 A-units, and 1,483 cabless B-units, were built for service in the United States, Canada, and Mexico. Also built were 371 FP7 A-units—the

EMD F7A SPECIFICATIONS

Type: Diesel-electric

Manufacturer: EMD

Years Built: 1949-1953

Wheel Arrangement: B-B

Engine: EMD 567B diesel

Output: 1,500 horsepower

Tractive Effort: Various, depending on gear ratio

Max. Operating Speed: 102 mph with 56:21 gearing

Weight: 230,000 lbs. (nominal, depending on options)

Overall Length: 50 ft. 8 in.

passenger variation of the F7 with a slightly longer car body having room for a large steam generator.

In 1954, EMD revamped its locomotive line with ten new models featuring improved equipment. With this change, the F9 supplanted the F7, and was offered until 1960, by which time the car-body style of locomotive had largely fallen out of favor. Technologically, the F9 was distinguished from the F7 by the 16-567C diesel-engine rated at 1,750 horsepower, and used a more advanced traction motor. Overall, the F9 was a much less common model than the F3 or F7. Large buyers of the model included Louisville & Nashville, Milwaukee Road, Northern Pacific, Rio Grande, and Santa Fe. EMD's FP9 passenger version was built for railroads in Canada and Mexico, as well as Saudi Arabia, but totaled just eighty-six units. The F9 body style was almost the same as late-built F7s, but there is an additional side louver between the cab door and first porthole window. The F9 used a flush headlight design instead of the rounded lip characteristic of earlier F models.

Although the numbers of EMD F-units began to wane in the late 1960s, when railroads traded them back for newer and more powerful road switchers, some F7s and F9s have survived. A few remain on short lines and as power for railroad executive business trains, and they are common in museums and on tourist railroads.

ABOVE: EMD's F3 went through several different body phases during its four-year production run, and this locomotive shows an early phase with air-intake vents covered by wire. *Brian Solomon*

OPPOSITE: Wabash's F7A No. 1189, built by General Motors Canadian subsidiary at London, Ontario, has been preserved and restored by the Monticello Railway Museum at Monticello, Illinois. *Brian Solomon*

ALCO-GE PA

The Alco-GE PA frequently has been deemed the most attractive American diesel of all time, exemplified by a handsome streamlined design featuring a six-foot-long nose. Introduced in 1946, this was Alco's post-war road passenger diesel intended to compete with EMD's successful E7. Typical of Alco's immediate postwar diesels, PA/PBs used General Electric electrical equipment and had joint Alco/GE builder plates reflecting the close relationship between the two companies. Its styling treatment, similar to Alco's freight service FA/FB models, was the genius of GE's designer Raymond E. Patten, who believed that the locomotive's powerful appearance would aid sales.

The PA1 was powered by a single turbocharged 244 engine rated at 2,000 horsepower and rode on a pair of A1A trucks. In 1950, PA2 was introduced with a 2,250 horsepower rating. In total, Alco built 297 PA/PB units for sixteen railways in the United States. The last surviving PAs were former Santa Fe units, bought by Delaware & Hudson in the late 1960s and sold to Mexico in the late 1970s. In 2000, two PAs were repatriated; one has been privately restored to resemble an engine that worked for Nickel Plate Road.

ALCO PA1 SPECIFICATIONS

Type: Diesel-electric road passenger

Manufacturer: Alco

Years Built: 1946-1949

Wheel Arrangement: A1A-A1A

Engine: Alco 16-244

Output: 2,000 horsepower

Tractive Effort: 24,000 lbs. continuous tractive (with 58:25 gearing)

Max. Operating Speed: 117 mph (with 58:25 gearing)

Weight: 303,000 (depending on options)

Overall Length: 65 ft. 8 in.

Lehigh Valley RR Alco PA is exchanged for a Pennsylvania Railroad GG1 electric at Newark, New Jersey, on May 10, 1959. *Richard Jay Solomon*

New York short line and tourist line Saratoga & North Creek has a pair of former Bangor & Aroostook BL2 diesels on its roster. *Dan Howard*

EMD BL2

In the 1940s, Electro-Motive emerged as the dominant American locomotive manufacturer. Initially, most of its production was focused on three basic types: the E-unit for long-distance passenger trains, the F-unit for general road service, and switchers. One exception to this was its curious looking branch-line locomotive that was one of its first attempts at selling a road-switcher type.

The semi-streamlined car body combined most of the equipment of the model F3 road diesels while providing some of advantages associated with switchers, such as a bidirectional cab with better views of the tracks and footboards to aid with yard work. EMD built a lone demonstrator in 1948—model BL1—followed by fifty-eight production-built BL2s. This model was only built for thirteen months and was effectively replaced in EMD's catalog by the less elegant, but more practical model GP7, introduced in 1949. Several BL2s survive, including a former Western Maryland engine as a static display at the Baltimore & Ohio Railroad Museum in Baltimore, former Bangor & Aroostook units serving New York's Saratoga & Creek, and Pennsylvania's Stourbridge Railroad, where they are primarily retained for tourist train services.

EMD BL2 SPECIFICATIONS

Type: Diesel-electric road switcher

Manufacturer: EMD

Years Built: 1948-1949

Wheel Arrangement: B-B

Engine: EMD 16-567B

Output: 1,500 horsepower

Tractive Effort: Depends on gear ratio

Max. Operating Speed: Depends on gear ratio

Weight: 260,000 lbs.

Overall Length: NA

EMD GP7, GP9, AND GP18

In EMD parlance, the letters GP stood for *general purpose* and were pronounced like the name of the common military automobile Jeep. Although EMD was relatively late to offer a road-switcher model, soon after the GP's introduction in 1949 this model became one of the best-selling locomotives in North America. Railroads recognized that they could get a more versatile locomotive for less money and embraced the road switcher. The GP offered flexibility and ultimately allowed railroads to take better advantage of the building-block principle of locomotive assignment, which allowed a railroad to adjust consists with as many diesel units as it needed.

Internally, the GP7 shared most major components with the F7, but lacked the exterior streamlining. Since every GP unit was bidirectional, the arrangement of locomotives in a consist was unimportant, unlike with unidirectional cab-units and cabless B-units that had faced a variety of limitations relating to the placement and direction of the individual unit within a consist.

GP9 SPECIFICATIONS

Type: Diesel-electric road switcher

Manufacturer: EMD

Years Built: 1954-1963

Wheel Arrangement: B-B

Engine: EMD 16-567C

Output: 1,750 horsepower

Tractive Effort: 44,000 lbs. at 12 mph (varied with gearing options)

Max. Operating Speed: 65 mph with 62:15 gearing

Weight: 244,000- 248,000 lbs. (varied depending on options)

Overall Length: 56 ft. 2 in.

ABOVE: A former Boston & Maine GP9 in Guilford Rail System paint works a GRS freight at East Deerfield Yard in Massachusetts. *Brian Solomon*

OPPOSITE: Maine Central GP7 573 has been preserved and restored to its traditional appearance (albeit with some modern equipment such as ditch lights). *Dan Howard*

Norfolk & Western 620, preserved at the North Carolina Transportation Museum in Spencer, presents an example of GP9 as built after October 1957. *Brian Solomon*

Like its cab-unit cousin Model F7, the GP7 was powered by a 16-cylinder 567 engine rated at 1,500 horsepower. In 1954, EMD upgraded its entire locomotive line to include a variety of equipment improvements. At that time, the GP9 replaced the GP7, and over the next decade it became the most common locomotive on North American rails with more than four thousand units built. The most significant change with the more-reliable GP9 was increased power: its 16-567C engine was rated at 1,750 horsepower.

There were several standard EMD road-switcher variations. One option was for dynamic brakes (locomotives so-equipped are easily distinguished by the braking grids in the bulged housing at the top center of the long hood, capped by a large cooling fan). Railroads had the choice of designating either short hood or long hood for the front of the locomotive, and could order locomotives with dual controls for ease of operation in either direction. For passenger operations, a steam generator could be fitted in the short hood. A few railroads ordered GPs with electric lighting equipment located in a squared-off box at the end of the long hood. During GP9 production, EMD added the low-short hood as an option, which gave crews better forward visibility. Pennsylvania Railroad, Santa Fe, and Union Pacific ordered cabless B-unit GPs.

The GP9 and the GP18 have more similarities than differences. Externally they look almost the same. One of the few external changes introduced with the GP18 and GP20 was the new style of radiator intake vent covering consisting of rows of horizontal bars with a prominent top-mounted drip guard. The GP7 and many GP9s featured a flush diagonal wire mesh. A more significant change came with the introduction of a new model diesel engine, the 16-567D1, rated at 1,800 horsepower. Despite overall improvements, the GP18 didn't sell as well, largely because by the time of its introduction in 1959 most railroads had completed dieselization and the frenzied period of locomotive buying that began after World War II had ended. In fact, EMD intended to boost sales for GP18s by encouraging railroads to trade back their older units. For example, Boston & Maine traded in its small fleet of BL2s for a half-dozen low-nose GP18s.

EMD's sound road-switcher design, famous for durability and flexibility, has led to an exceptional service record. Many GP7 and GP9s have been in service for more than six decades, most outlasting their original owners—railroad companies that were swept away years ago by mergers.

However, a GP9 working today is unlikely to be in its factory condition. Among the advantages of Electro-Motive's design philosophy was the ease of upgrading individual locomotives with key components that were interchangeable. Externally, railroads modified the locomotives by installing improved headlights and new horns, moving bells, replacing handrails and grab irons, and also adding new equipment such as window frames, exhaust stack-spark arrestors, warning lights, and after-market air filtration ducts.

Rebuilding or remanufacturing programs implemented significant changes, such as redesigned airflow systems, significant upgrading of the locomotive electrical system, and in some situations the replacement of the original 567 engine. Where some GPs were rebuilt with more modern, or modified, variations of the 16-567 engine, others benefitted from the 1960s-era 16-645 engine, while a few were fitted with third-party engines, including Caterpillar. In recent years, manufacture of Genset locomotives has often favored old EMD GP platforms as a solid base for modern advanced equipment.

External modifications have often resulted in lowering of the short hood, changing the engine exhaust system from two to four stacks, and removing dynamic braking equipment, including blanking-over dynamic brake grids, blisters and fans. Santa Fe was among railroads that installed more spacious cabs to GPs.

A few unmodified GPs survive on large railroads, while numerous more-or-less as-built units have been preserved at museums and tourist lines across the continent.

ALCO RS-3

Alco's model RS-3 was an improvement on its original road switcher design of 1941 (see RS-1, page 174). During World War II, Alco refined new diesel engine designs, and after the war it introduced variations of its 244 diesel for most new road locomotives. From late 1945, 1,500 12-cylinder 244s were produced, and in 1946 Alco also introduced a new semi-streamlined four-motor road-switcher, designated RS-2. Alco increased its B-B road locomotive output from 1,500 to 1,600 horsepower in 1950, so a few late-build RS-2s were rated at 1,600 horsepower. Later that year, Alco introduced its RS-3, a move that reflected the increased output while offering other design refinements.

The RS-3 was built at a time when road diesel purchases shifted to favor road-switcher models instead of full car body types (such as Alco FA and EMD F7 models). The road switcher was cheaper and more versatile, offering bidirectional operation and easier maintenance.

The RS-3 was in production from 1950 and 1956, during which time Alco built 1,265 RS-3s for American operation, with additional units constructed by its Canadian affiliate, Montreal Locomotive Works. Many Northeastern lines bought RS-3s, including Boston & Maine, Central Railroad of New Jersey, Delaware & Hudson, Erie Railroad, Lehigh Valley, New York Central, New Haven, Pennsylvania Railroad, and Western Maryland. The type was also bought

ALCO RS-3 SPECIFICATIONS

Type: Diesel-electric road switcher

Manufacturer: Alco

Years Built: 1950-1956

Wheel Arrangement: B-B

Engine: Alco 12-244

Output: 1,600 horsepower

Continuous Tractive Effort: Depends on gearing

Max. Operating Speed: 92 mph with 62:21 gearing

Weight: 240,000-250,000 lbs.

Overall Length: 56 ft.

Restored New York Central RS-3 leads an Adirondack Scenic Railroad excursion on former home rails near Thendara, New York. *Brian Solomon*

A pair of Delaware-Lackawanna RS-3s work at Bridge 60 in Scranton, Pennsylvania, on September 17, 2007. *Brian Solomon*

by lines in the Midwest and South, but was relatively uncommon in the West. Similar-looking models were also sold for export.

Alco discontinued the RS3 when it introduced its new 251 diesel for road service, with the RS11 effectively replacing it in their American catalog. Difficulties with the 244 engine design resulted in shorter service lives for many Alco diesels.

A few railroads rebuilt RS-3s using other diesel prime movers. Penn Central and Conrail rebuilt many RS-3s using the more reliable Electro-Motive 12-567 engine largely salvaged from retired E-units. Because this EMD engine was taller than the Alco 244, many rebuilt RS-3s required an unsightly bulge on the long hood. During the mid-1970s, Morrison-Knudsen rebuilt a few Delaware & Hudson RS-3s with the Alco 251 engine, lowering the short hood to give crews an improved forward view. While the vast majority of RS-3s were traded for new diesels or scrapped, a few survive today on short lines and in railroad museums.

On April 18, 1992, a trio of six-motor EMD SD9s work a train at Ridge on California's Northwestern Pacific route. *Brian Solomon*

EMD SD7/SD9

In the 1950s, EMD's four-axle GP emerged as a universal locomotive, the jack of all trades, while its six-axle cousin was reserved for "Special Duty"—thus the SD designation. Alco and Baldwin had offered high-tractive-effort six-motor road switchers in the 1940s, but it wasn't until 1952 that EMD brought out its SD7. Horsepower output was the same as its GP7 "General Purpose" model, but the SD7 offered greater tractive effort and better weight distribution. In 1954, EMD replaced the SD7 with the SD9, rated at 1,750 horsepower, which, like other new models, employed the new 567C diesel.

Southern Pacific had been a large buyer of SD7s and proved to be the largest buyer of SD9s. SP crews liked the smooth ride offered by six-axle trucks and called these engines "Cadillacs" after the luxury General Motors automobile noted for its smooth-riding characteristics. Many of these locomotives were rebuilt at SP's Sacramento (California) Shops, which prolonged their service lives. The SD9s were common nationally and a few can still be found earning their keep; several have been preserved in railway museums.

SD9 SPECIFICATIONS

Type: Diesel-electric road switcher

Manufacturer: EMD

Years Built: 1954-1959

Wheel Arrangement: C-C

Engine: EMD 16-567C

Output: 2,000 horsepower

Tractive Effort: 67,500 lbs. at 8 mph

Max. Operating Speed: 65 mph with 62:15 gearing

Weight: 324,000 lbs.

Overall Length: 60 ft. 8 in.

NEW HAVEN FL9

A specialized and very unusual Electro-Motive Division F-unit variation was the model FL9 built exclusively for the New York, New Haven & Hartford Railroad (New Haven Railroad). Sixty were delivered between 1956 and 1960. The FL9 was a hybrid diesel-electric/electric designed to operate either as a normal diesel-electric using an onboard 16-567C diesel engine, or as an electric locomotive drawing current from line-side third rail. Since the locomotive needed to make the electrical transition from diesel-electric to electric while rolling along at speed, it required additional electrical equipment. As a result, the FL9 was a full 8 feet longer than the F9.

Unlike typical F-units, the FL9 has B-A1A trucks; its rear three-axle A1A Flexicoil truck (center axle unpowered) was necessary to accommodate weight restrictions on approach to Grand Central Terminal. New Haven's FL9s went to Penn-Central, then Amtrak and Conrail. Commuter operator Metro-North inherited many of the locomotives for New York City suburban services, where some worked until 2009. Several survive in museums and on tourist lines, including New Haven 2059, which was the very last F-unit built by General Motors and is stored at the Railroad Museum of New England pending restoration.

NEW HAVEN FL9 SPECIFICATIONS

Type: passenger diesel-electric/third rail electric

Manufacturer: EMD

Years Built: 1956-1960

Wheel Arrangement: B-A1A

Engine: 16- 567C or 16-567D1

Output: 1,750 horsepower (based on 567C used for first 30 built)

Tractive Effort: NA

Max. Operating Speed: NA

Weight: 66,400 lbs.

Overall Length: 58 ft. 8 in.

On June 22, 1985, a freshly rebuilt Connecticut Department of Transportation FL9 2019 leads an excursion at New Haven, Connecticut.
Brian Solomon

Genesee Valley Transportation C-425 2461 is lettered for its Delaware-Lackawanna line. Here it works upgrade at Cresco on the line over Pocono Summit. *Brian Solomon*

ALCO
CENTURY SERIES

The final line of locomotive from long-time locomotive manufacturer, Alco, was its elegant-looking Century Series. It was offered in reaction to increased competition from its one-time partner GE, and to new and improved high-output models offered by EMD, GE, and others. Over the next six years, Alco offered a number of four- and six-motor models with incrementally more horsepower to match models offered by its competition. Series models used a new system of model designation that logically described powered axles and horsepower. It prefaced each model with "C" (for Century) followed by a three-digit number: the first digit indicated the number of powered axles, the second and third digits inferred approximate horsepower output. Alco's Canadian affiliate Montreal Locomotive Works built similar versions of the Century Series for Canadian roads.

C-636 EXAMPLE SPECIFICATIONS

Type: C-C, diesel-electric road locomotive

Manufacturer: Alco

Years Built: 1967-1968

Engine: Alco 16-251E

Output: 3,600 horsepower

Tractive Effort: Continuous 79,500 lbs. at 12 mph

Max. Operating Speed: NA

Weight: NA

Overall Length: 69 ft. 6 in.

EMD DDA40X

During the 1960s, in an attempt to meet Union Pacific's exceptional thirst for diesel power, American diesel manufacturers developed exceptionally high-horsepower diesel road-switchers using dual-prime movers with powered eight axles—in effect a pair of four-motor locomotives on one frame. EMD's used DD wheel arrangement (since a two-axle truck is designed B, a three-axle is a C, logically, a four-axle is D). In 1969, Union Pacific took renewed interest in double-diesels, and ordered forty-seven specially built model DDA40X locomotives from EMD. Deemed the largest and most powerful commercial diesel-locomotives ever built, they are powered by pair of 16-cylinder 645E3 diesels designed to produce 6,600 horsepower. Significantly, a DDA40X produced more horsepower in the highest throttle position than comparable pairs of single-engine types by working its engines at higher maximum engine rpm. Externally, the model featured a cowl cab style with a full-width nose and large two-piece windshield that anticipated the now-common North American Safety Cab. The year 1969 represented the centennial of the completion of the first transcontinental railroad, so UP's DDA40X's were numbered in the 6900 series and termed "Centennials." More than a dozen have been preserved, and UP 6936 has been maintained as part of the railroad's Heritage Fleet.

EMD DDA40X SPECIFICATIONS

Type: Double diesel-electric

Manufacturer: EMD

Years Built: 1969-1971

Engine: 2 EMD 16-645E3 diesels

Output: 6,600 horsepower

Tractive Effort: NA

Max. Operating Speed: 90 mph (estimated)

Weight: 522,000 lbs. (estimated)

Overall Length: 98 ft. 5 in.

The great length of Union Pacific's DDA40X is evident in this photograph at the Honeymoon Tunnels in California's Feather River Canyon. UP 6936 leads the historic Electro-Motive FT set on its way to Sacramento, California. *Brian Solomon*

Historic Streetcars

PETER WITTS

The widely built Peter Witt was a steel-body, center-door streetcar noted for its early use of the pay-as-you-enter system, where passengers paid their fare to the motorman, eliminating the need for a conductor. Exiting passengers used the center door to minimize delays during stops. The car type was named for its designer, the Cleveland Street Railway commissioner who originated the car arrangement about 1915. Peter Witt types were widely built by a number of manufacturers, including J.G Brill in Philadelphia and the St. Louis Car Company in the United States, and Canadian Car & Foundry, Ottawa Car Company, and Preston Car Company in Canada. Philadelphia operated Peter Witts until the late 1950s.

Toronto had Canada's most extensive fleet, 350 powered cars plus trailers. The trailers were the last of their kind in North American, operating until 1954; powered Peter Witts survived on Toronto streets until 1963, and the last cars weren't retired until 1965. Toronto Transit Commission 2766 was restored and retained for excursions.

The Peter Witt was adopted in Italy in the late 1920s, and number of former Milan Peter Witts have been imported to the United States for historic service, notably in San Francisco, where they work daily on the F-Market route.

ABOVE: A former Milan car catches the sun on the Embarcadero in San Francisco. *Brian Solomon*

OPPOSITE: A vintage MBTA PCC works the Mattapan-Ashmont line. *Brian Solomon*

BIRNEY CARS

The lightweight steel-body single-truck Birney Safety Car was developed by Charles Oliver Birney about 1910, and was a common sight on many North American Transit Systems. By employing automated equipment to allow for safe one-man operation, the Birney car offered an efficient low-capacity design for use on lightly traveled lines. Later, a double-truck lightweight Birney car was introduced. Birney cars were built by several established American streetcar manufacturers, including: J.G. Brill of Philadelphia; Cincinnati Car Company; St., Louis Car Company; and the Wason Car Company of Springfield, Massachusetts. The Ottawa Car Manufacturing Company supplied cars to Canadian street railways.

Fort Collins, Colorado, was the last American city to regularly work single-truck Birney Cars. While regular service ended in 1951, Car 21 was preserved locally and in the 1980s it was restored for historic service. Birneys are preserved in a number of museums around the country, including a Sacramento Northern single-truck car preserved at the Western Railway Museum in Rio Vista, Californi, and Johnstown Traction Company 311 (a double-truck car) at Pennsylvania's Rockhill Furnace Trolley Museum. The Gomaco Trolley Company of Ida Grove, Iowa, specializes in building replica cars for historic services and has supplied recreated Birney cars to several cities, including Charlotte, North Carolina; Little Rock, Arkansas; Memphis, Tennessee; and Tampa, Florida.

Fort Collins Birney Safety Car 21 provides a link with history as it works 1.5 miles of street trackage. *Jack May*

PCC CARS

The Presidents' Conference Committee car was an advanced lightweight streetcar created in the 1930s in an effort to strengthen the role of the American street railway. It was exemplified by its streamlined body, which was the work of automotive engineer John W. Hession Jr. In 1934, a demonstration model worked Chicago streets before traveling to Cleveland, Ohio, for display at the American Transit Association convention. A number of nominal changes were made to the car before its commercial debut in Brooklyn, New York, in 1936.

By 1952, an estimated five thousand PCCs had been built for dozens of transit systems across North America. Fundamental elements of PCC technology were licensed to foreign manufacturers, although many overseas PCCs looked quite different than their American cousins. American PCCs had a number of variations, including different window arrangements, single- and double-end types, and cars built for various different track gauges.

After World War II, the PCC was the dominant North American streetcar, but its popularity coincided with the rapid decline of most remaining streetcar systems; as

San Francisco Muni PCC 1056 is painted as a tribute to the cars that served Kansas City Public Service. *Brian Solomon*

a result the PCC was often the last type of trolley on a city's streets. Despite near extinction, the American street railway never completely vanished, and PCCs held the fort in a number of cities until the light rail revival began in the 1980s with new cars taking over. Several American cities have continued to operate restored PCCs in regular service and these classics remain popular with the traveling public. Boston operates them on its Mattapan-Ashmont line—an isolated trolley extension of MBTA's Red Line rapid transit route. San Francisco's Muni revived the PCC in the 1990s, and has the most colorful fleet. In addition to cars painted in traditional San Francisco schemes, many of Muni's thirty-two cars are painted in a classic transit liveries intended to represent cars from one-time PCC operating cities, including Baltimore, Birmingham, Chicago, Cincinnati, Dallas, Detroit, El Paso, Kansas City, Louisville, Kentucky, Newark, New Jersey, Toronto, and Washington DC These are routinely operated on the F-Market route. In 2005, Philadelphia's SEPTA used modernized PCCs to revive the long-dormant number 15 streetcar route along Girard Avenue. Transit systems in San Diego, California, and Kenosha, Wisconsin, also work PCC heritage cars. In addition, there are dozens of restored PCCs at railway museums across North America.

ABOVE: MBTA PCC's painted in vintage "traction orange" pass at Central Avenue in Milton, Massachusetts, in May 2015. *Brian Solomon*

OPPOSITE: MBTA maintains a fleet of ten vintage PCCs for service on the Mattapan-Ashmont Red Line extension. *Brian Solomon*

BIBLIOGRAPHY

BOOKS

Alexander, Edwin P. Iron Horses. New York, 1941.

———. American Locomotives. New York, 1950.

Armstrong, John H. The Railroad—What it is, What it Does. Simmons-Boardman Publishing Corp. Omaha, NE. 1982.

Asay, Jeff S. Track and Time—An Operational History of the Western Pacific Railroad through   Timetables and Maps. Portola, CA, 2006

Bean, W. L. Twenty Years of Electrical Operation on the New York, New Haven and Hartford Railroad. East Pittsburgh, PA, 1927.

Bell, J. Snowdon. The Early Motive Power of the Baltimore and Ohio Railroad. New York, 1912.

Bezilla, Michael. Electric Traction on the Pennsylvania Railroad 1895–1968. State College, PA, 1981.

Bruce, Alfred W. The Steam Locomotive in America. New York, 1952.

Burgess, George, H., and Miles C. Kennedy, Centennial History of the Pennsylvania Railroad. Philadelphia, 1949.

Burke, Davis. The Southern Railway—Road of the Innovators. The University of North Carolina Press, Chapel Hill, NC, 1985.

Bush, Donald, J. The Streamlined Decade. New York, 1975.

Churella, Albert, J. From Steam to Diesel. Princeton, NJ. 1998.

Conrad, J. David. The Steam Locomotive Directory of North America. Vols. I & II. Polo, IL:
Transportation Trails, 1988.

Cudahy, Brian J. Box Boats. New York, 2006.

DeBoer, David J. Piggyback and Containers. San Marino, CA, 1992.

Del Grosso, Robert C. Burlington Northern 1980–1991 Annual. Denver, 1991.

DeNevi, Don. The Western Pacific—Railroading Yesterday, Today and Tomorrow. Seattle, WA, 1978.

Dixon, Thomas W. Jr., Chesapeake & Ohio—Superpower to Diesels. Newton, NJ, 1984.

Doherty, Timothy Scott, and Brian Solomon. Conrail. MBI Publishing, St. Paul, MN, 2004.

Dolzall, Gary W. and Stephen F. Dolzall. Baldwin Diesel Locomotives. Milwaukee, WI, 1984.

———. Monon—The Hoosier Line. Glendale, CA, 1987.

Dorsey, Edward Bates. English and American Railroads Compared. New York, 1887.

Drury, George H. The Historical Guide to North American Railroads. Waukesha, WI, 1985.

———. The Train Watcher's Guide to North American Railroads. Waukesha, WI, 1992.

———. Guide to North American Steam Locomotives. Waukesha, WI, 1993.

Dubin, Arthur D. Some Classic Trains. Milwaukee, WI, 1964.

———. More Classic Trains. Milwaukee, WI, 1974.

Dunscomb, Guy, L. A Century of Southern Pacific Steam Locomotives. Modesto, CA, 1963.

Farrington, S. Kip, Jr. Railroading from the Head End. New York, 1943.

———. Railroads at War. New York, 1944.

———. Railroading from the Rear End. New York, 1946.

———. Railroads of Today. New York, 1949.

———. Railroading the Modern Way. New York, 1951.

———. Railroads of the Hour. New York, 1958.

Garmany, John B. Southern Pacific Dieselization. Edmonds, WA, 1985.

Glischinski, Steve. Burlington Northern and its Heritage. Andover, NJ, and Osceola, WI, 1996.

————. Santa Fe Railway. Osceola, WI, 1997.

Gruber, John. Railroad History in a Nutshell. Madison, WI, 2009

————. Railroad Preservation in a Nutshell. Madison, WI, 2011

Gruber, John, and Brian Solomon. The Milwaukee Road's Hiawathas. St. Paul, MN, 2006.

Hampton, Taylor. The Nickel Plate Road. Cleveland, OH, 1947.

Harris, Ken. World Electric Locomotives. Jane's Publishing Co., London, 1981.

Haut, F. J. G. The History of the Electric Locomotive. London, 1969.

————. The Pictorial History of Electric Locomotives. Cranbury, NJ, 1970.

Heimburger, Donald J. Wabash. River Forest, IL, 1984.

Hilton, George W. American Narrow Gauge Railroads. Stanford, CA, 1990.

Holton, James L. The Reading Railroad: History of a Coal Age Empire. Vol. I & II. Garrigues House, Laurys Station, PA, 1992.

Hofsommer, Don. L. Southern Pacific 1900–1985. College Station, TX, 1986.

Karig, Martin Robert, III. Coal Cars—The First Three Hundred Years. University of Scranton Press, Scranton, PA, 2007.

Keilty, Edmund. Interurbans Without Wires. Glendale, CA, 1979.

Kiefer, P. W. A Practical Evaluation of Railroad Motive Power. New York, 1948.

Kirkland, John, F. Dawn of the Diesel Age. Interurban Press, Pasadena, CA, 1994.

Kirkland, John, F. The Diesel Builders Vols. I, II, and III. Glendale, CA, 1983.

Klein, Maury. History of the Louisville & Nashville Railroad. New York, 1972.

————. Union Pacific, Vols. I & II. New York, 1989.

Kratville, William, and Harold E. Ranks. Motive Power of the Union Pacific. Omaha, NE, 1958.

Kobus, Ken, and Gary Rauch. Pennsy's Conemaugh Division. The Pennsylvania Railroad Technical and Historical Society, Upper Darby, PA, 2007.

Lee, Randall B. Intermodal Modeler's Guide. Aurora, CO, 1997.

LeMassena, Robert A. Colorado's Mountain Railroads. Golden, CO, 1963.

————. Rio Grande to the Pacific. Denver, 1974.

Leopard, John. Wisconsin Central Heritage Vol. II. La Mirada, CA, 2008.

Levinson, Marc. The Box. Princeton, NJ, 2006.

Lloyd, Gordon, Jr. and Louis A. Marre. Conrail Motive Power Review, Vol. 1. Glendale, CA, 1992.

Malone, Michael P. James J. Hill, Empire Builder of the Northwest. Norman, OK, 1996.

Marre, Louis A. and Jerry A. Pinkepank. The Contemporary Diesel Spotter's Guide. Milwaukee, WI, 1985.

Marre, Louis, A. Diesel Locomotives: The First 50 Years. Waukesha, WI, 1995.

Marre, Louis A., and Paul K. Withers. The Contemporary Diesel Spotter's Guide, Year 2000 Edition. Halifax, PA, 2000.

McDonald, Charles W. Diesel Locomotive Rosters. Milwaukee, WI, 1982.

McDonnell, Greg. U-Boats: General Electric Diesel Locomotives. Toronto, ON, 1994.

McMillan, Joe. Santa Fe's Diesel Fleet. Burlingame, CA, 1975.

Middleton, William D. When the Steam Railroads Electrified. Milwaukee, WI, 1974.

————. Landmarks on the Iron Road. Bloomington, IN, 1999.

Middleton, William D., with George M. Smerk and Roberta L. Diehl. Encyclopedia of North American Railroads. Indiana University Press,

Bloomington and Indianapolis, IN, 2007.

Miller, Donald L. and Richard E. Sharpless. The Kingdom of Coal. University of Pennsylvania Press, Philadelphia, PA, 1985.

Mika, Nick., with Helma Mika. Railways of Canada. Toronto and Montreal, ON, 1972.

Morgan, David P. Steam's Finest Hour. Milwaukee, WI, 1959.

————. Canadian Steam! Milwaukee, WI, 1961.

Murray, Tom. Canadian National Railway. St. Paul, MN, 2004.

————. Western Pacific—The Last Transcontinental Railroad. Colorado Rail Annual No. 27. Golden, CO, 2006.

Parker, Thomas H., III, and Paul K. Withers with Kenneth M. Ardinger. CSX Transportation Locomotive Directory 2004-2005. Withers Publishing, Halifax, PA, 2005.

Ransome-Wallis, P. World Railway Locomotives. New York, 1959.

Reck, Franklin M. On Time. Electro-Motive Division of General Motors, 1948.

Reck, Franklin M. The Dilworth Story. New York, 1954.

Riddell, Doug. From the Cab. Pasadena, CA, 1999.

Roberts, Earl W. with David P Stremes. The Canadian Trackside Guide 1997. Bytown Railway Society, Inc., Ottawa, ON, 1997

Rosenbaum, Joel, and Tom Gallo. NJ Transit Rail Operations. Railpace Company, Inc., Piscataway, NJ, 1996.

Saunders, Richard, Jr. The Railroad Mergers and the Coming of Conrail. Westport, CT, 1978.

————. Merging Lines: American Railroads 1900–1970. DeKalb, IL, 2001.

————. Main Lines: American Railroads 1970–2002. DeKalb, IL, 2003.

Saylor, Roger B. The Railroads of Pennsylvania. Pennsylvania State University Press, University Park, PA, 1964.

Schafer, Mike, and Brian Solomon. Pennsylvania Railroad. Minneapolis, MN, 2009.

Schneider, Paul D. GM's Geeps—The General Purpose Diesel. Waukesha, WI, 2001.

Schwandl, Robert. Subways & Light Rail in the U.S.A. Vols 1, 2 and 3. Verlag, Berlin, DE, 2012.

Shaughnessy, Jim. Delaware & Hudson. Howell North Books, Berkeley, CA, 1967.

————. The Rutland Road, 2nd edition. Syracuse, NY, 1997.

Sinclair, Angus. Development of the Locomotive Engine. New York, 1907.

Smalley, Eugene V. History of the Northern Pacific Railroad. New York, 1883.

Snopek, Joseph R. with Robert A. La May. Diesels to Park Avenue—The FL9 Story. New England Rails Publishing, Granby, MA, 1997.

Solomon, Brian. Trains of the Old West. New York, 1998.

————. The American Steam Locomotive. Osceola, WI, 1998.

————. The American Diesel Locomotive. Osceola, WI, 2000.

————. Super Steam Locomotives. Osceola, WI, 2000.

————. Locomotive. Osceola, WI, 2001.

————. Railway Masterpieces: Celebrating the World's Greatest Trains, Stations and Feats of Engineering. Iola, WI, 2002.

————. Electric Locomotives. Voyageur Press, St. Paul, MN, 2003.

————. GE Locomotives. Voyageur Press, St. Paul, MN, 2003.

————. Amtrak. Voyageur Press, St. Paul, MN, 2004.

————. Burlington Northern Santa Fe Railway. Voyageur Press, St. Paul, MN, 2005.

————. Southern Pacific Passenger Trains. Voyageur Press, St. Paul, MN, 2005.

————. CSX. Voyageur Press, St. Paul, MN, 2005.

————. EMD Locomotives. Voyageur Press, St. Paul, MN, 2006.

————. Railroads of Pennsylvania. Voyageur Press, Minneapolis, MN, 2008.

————. Alco Locomotives. Voyageur Press, Minneapolis, MN, 2009.

————. Vintage Diesel Power. Voyageur Press, Minneapolis, MN, 2010.

————. Electro-Motive E-Units and F-Units. Voyageur Press, Minneapolis, MN, 2011.

————. Modern Diesel Power. Voyageur Press, Minneapolis, MN, 2011.

————. The Majesty of Big Steam. Voyageur Press, Minneapolis, MN, 2015.

Solomon, Brian, and Mike Schafer. New York Central Railroad. Osceola, WI, 1999.

Staff, Virgil. D-Day on the Western Pacific. Glendale, CA, 1982.

Staufer, Alvin F. Steam Power of the New York Central System, Volume 1. Medina, OH, 1961.

————. C&O Power. Carrollton, OH, 1965.

————. Pennsy Power III. Medina, OH, 1993.

Staufer, Alvin F. and Edward L. May. New York Central's Later Power. Medina, OH, 1981.

Steinbrenner, Richard T. The American Locomotive Company—A Centennial Remembrance. Warren, NJ, 2003.

Stover, John F. The Life and Decline of the American Railroad. New York, 1970.

————. History of the New York Central Railroad. New York, 1975.

————. The Routledge Historical Atlas of the American Railroads. New York, 1999.

Strapac, Joseph A. Southern Pacific Motive Power Annual 1971. Burlingame, CA, 1971.

————. Southern Pacific Review 1981. Huntington Beach, CA, 1982.

————. Southern Pacific Review 1953-1985. Huntington Beach, CA, 1986.

Stretton, Clement E. The Development of the Locomotive—A Popular History 1803-1896. London, 1896.

Swengel, Frank M. The American Steam Locomotive: Volume 1, Evolution. Davenport, IA, 1967.

Talbot, F. A. Railway Wonders of the World, Volumes 1 & 2. London, 1914.

Teichmoeller, John. Pennsylvania Railroad Steel Open Hopper Cars. Highland Stations, Inc., Aurora, CO, 2000.

Thompson, Gregory Lee. The Passenger Train in the Motor Age. Columbus, OH, 1993.

————. Short History of American Railways. Chicago, IL, 1925.

Trewman, H. F. Electrification of Railways. London, 1920.

Turner, Gregg M., and Melancthon W. Jacobus. Connecticut Railroads. The Connecticut Historical Society, Hartford, CT, 1989.

Vance, James E., Jr. The North American Railroad. Baltimore, MD, 1995.

Walker, Mike. Steam Powered Video's Comprehensive Railroad Atlas of North America—North East U.S.A. Steam Powered Publishing, Feaversham, Kent, UK, 1993.

Webster, Neil. European Railways Motive Power. Vols 1 and 3. Metro Enterprises Ltd., Birstall, Batley, UK, 1995.

Weller, John, L. The New Haven Railroad—Its Rise and Fall. Hastings House, New York, 1969.

Westing, Frederic. Apex of the Atlantics. Milwaukee, WI, 1963.

————. Penn Station: Its Tunnels and Side Rodders. Seattle, WA, 1977.

White, John H., Jr. A History of the American Locomotive—Its Development: 1830–1880. Dover Publications, Mineola, NY, 1980.

————. The American Railroad Passenger Car, Vols. I & II. John Hopkins University Press, Baltimore, MD, 1978.

White, Roy V., and A. C. Loudon. Car Builders Dictionary. Simmons-Boardman, New York, 1916.

Wilner, Frank N. The Amtrak Story. Omaha, NE, 1994.

Williams, Gerry. Trains, Trolleys & Transit—A Guide to Philadelphia Area Rail Transit. Railpace Company Inc., Piscataway, NJ, 1998

Wilson, O. Meredith. The Denver and Rio Grande Project, 1870–1901. Salt Lake City, UT, 1982.

Winchester, Clarence. Railway Wonders of the World, Volumes 1 & 2. London, 1935.

Withers, Paul K. Conrail Motive Power Review 1986-1991. Halifax, PA, 1992.

————. Norfolk Southern Locomotive Directory 2001. Halifax, PA, 2001

Wright, Richard K. Southern Pacific Daylight. Thousand Oaks, CA, 1970.

Zimmermann, Karl R. Erie Lackawanna East. New York, 1975.

————. The Remarkable GG1. New York, 1977.

PERIODICALS

CTC Board, Ferndale, WA.

Diesel Era, Halifax, PA.

Diesel Railway Traction, supplement to Railway Gazette (UK). (merged into Railway Gazette)

Extra 2200 South, Cincinnati, OH.

Jane's Freight Containers, London.

Jane's World Railways, London.

Keystone Coal Buyers Manual, McGraw Hill Publishing Co.

Locomotive Cyclopedia, New York, 1922-1947. (no longer published)

Moody's Analyses of Investments, Part I—Steam Railroads, New York.

Pacific RailNews, Waukesha, WI. (no longer published)

Rail International, Brussels, BE.

Railroad History, formerly Railway and Locomotive Historical Society Bulletin, Boston, MA.

Official Guide to the Railways, New York.

Railway and Locomotive Engineering, New York. (no longer published)

Railway Age, Chicago and New York.

Railway Gazette, New York, 1870–1908. (no longer published)

Railway Mechanical Engineer 1925-1952 (no longer published)

Shoreliner, Grafton, Mass.

Southern Pacific Bullet, San Francisco, CA.

The Car and Locomotive Cyclopedia, Simmons-Boardman, Omaha, NE.

The Railway Gazette, London.

Traffic World, Washington, D.C.

TRAINS Magazine, Waukesha, WI.

Vintage Rails, Waukesha, WI. (no longer published)

BROCHURES, OPERATING MANUALS, TIMETABLES, RULE BOOKS

American Locomotive Co., General Electric Co. Operating Manual Model RS-3, Schenectady, NY, 1951.

American Locomotive Co., General Electric Co. Manual for Enginemen; 660-HP switcher, 1,000-HP switcher, 1,000-HP Road Switcher. Schenectady, NY.

Amtrak public timetables, 1971 to 2011.

Amtrak. AEM-7 AC Electric Locomotive Operator's Manual. 1999.

Ansaldobreda, Boston LRV, no date.

Ansaldobreda, Cleveland LRV, no date.

Ansaldobreda, Metro Los Angele LRV proposal, no date.

Ansaldobreda, San Francisco LRV, no date.

Baldwin Locomotive Works. Eight-Coupled Locomotives for Freight Service. Record No. 99. Philadelphia, 1920.

Burlington Northern Santa Fe Corporation. Annual Reports 1996–2004.

Canadian National. Current Issues, Diesel Unit Data. c. 1970.

Conrail. Pittsburgh Division, System Timetable No. 5. 1997.

CSX Transportation. Baltimore Division, Timetable No. 2. 1987.

General Electric. A New Generation For Increased Productivity. Erie, PA, 1987.

General Electric. Dash 8 Locomotive Line. No Date.

General Electric. GENESIS Series. 1993.

General Electric. Geneis Series 2 P32AC-DM Operating Manual. Erie, PA, 1998.

General Electric. Operating Manual DC Evolution Series Diesel-Electric Locomotive ES44DC. Erie, PA.

General Motors. Electro-Motive Division Operating Manual No. 2300. La Grange, IL, 1945.

General Motors. Electro-Motive Division Model F3 Operating Manual No. 2308B. La Grange, IL, 1948.

General Motors. Electro-Motive Division Model 567B Engine Maintenance Manual. La Grange, IL, 1948

General Motors. Electro-Motive Division, Diesel Locomotive Operating Manual No. 2312 for Model GP7 with Vapor Car Steam Generator. 2nd Edition. La Grange, IL, 1950.

General Motors. Electro-Motive Division Model F7 Operating Manual No. 2310. La Grange, IL, 1951.

General Motors. Electro-Motive Division Operating Manual No. 2316 for Model E9. La Grange, IL, 1954.

General Motors. Electro-Motive Division SD45 Operator's Manual. La Grange, IL, 1977.

General Motors. Electro-Motive Division F40PH-2C Operator's Manual. La Grange, IL, 1988.

General Motors. Electro-Motive Division SD70M Operator's Manual. La Grange, IL, 1994.

General Motors. Electro-Motive Division SD80MACLocomotive Operation Manual. La Grange, IL, 1996.

Gunderson. Maxi Stack I Technical Bulletin. No Date.

Gunderson. Maxi Stack III Technical Bulletin. No Date.

Gunderson. Huskie Stack 53' Container Car Technical Bulletin. No Date.

Kinkisharyo, Boston-MBTA: Green Line Technical Data. No Date.

Kinkisharyo, Dallas-Dallas Area Rapid Transit Technical Data. No Date.

Kinkisharyo, Hudson-Bergen Line-New Jersey Technical Data. No Date.

Kinkisharyo, Phoenix-Valley Metro Rail Technical Data. No Date.

Kinkisharyo, Santa Clara-Valley Transportation Technical Data. No Date.

Kinkisharyo, Seattle-Sound Transit Technical Data. No Date.

New York Central System. Rules for the Government of the Operating Department. 1937.

NORAC Operating Rules, 7th Edition. 2000.

Norfolk Southern, Condensed List and Descriptions of Locomotives. 1999.

Pennsylvania Railroad public timetables, 1942–1968.

Proceedings of the Institution of Mechanical Engineers. Diesel Locomotives for the Future. New York, 1987.

Siemens. ACS-64 Locomotive Familiarization and Orientation. 2013.

Southern Pacific Company. Public timetables, 1930 to 1958.

Steamtown National Historic Site. The Nation's Living Railroad Museum. No Date.

TTX Equipment Guide, TTX Company, Chicago, IL, 1997.

Union Pacific. System Timetable No. 7. 1983.

REPORTS AND UNPUBLISHED WORKS

Clemensen, A. Berle. Historic Research Study: Steamtown National Historic Site Pennsylvania. U.S. Department of the Interior, Denver, CO, 1988.

Chappell, Gordon. Flanged Wheels on Steel Rails—Cars of Steamtown. Unpublished.

Johnson, Ralph P., chief engineer. The Four Cylinder Duplex Locomotive as Built for the Pennsylvania Railroad. Presented in New York, May 1945. Published in Philadelphia, PA.

Johnson, Ralph P., chief engineer. Railroad Motive Power Trends. Presented November 1945. Published in Philadelphia, PA.

Meyer, C. W. Comments on Ralph P. Johnson's Paper, November 29, 1945. Presented November 1945. Published in Philadelphia, PA.

Warner, Paul T. The Story of the Baldwin Locomotive Works. Philadelphia, PA, 1935.

Warner, Paul T. Compound Locomotives. Presented in New York, April 14, 1939.

INDEX

ABOUT THE AUTHOR

Brian Solomon has authored more than sixty books, including *Railway Depots, Stations & Terminals*, *The Majesty of Big Steam*, *Alco Locomotives*, *North American Railroad Bridges*, *Amtrak*, *Railroad Signaling*, *Railway Masterpieces*, *The American Steam Locomotive*, and *America's Railroad Stations*. He served as the editor of *Pacific RailNews* for Pentrex Publishing in Waukesha, Wisconsin, for several years, before embarking on a career as a freelance author and photographer. His work has appeared in numerous railroad publications including: *TRAINS Magazine*, *Railfan & Railroad*, *Railway Age*, and *The Journal of the Irish Railway Record Society*. He produces a daily blog on railway photography at www.briansolomon.com/trackingthelight.